effortless

effortless

MAKE IT EASIER TO DO WHAT MATTERS MOST

GREG McKEOWN

3

Ebury Edge, an imprint of Ebury Publishing
One Embassy Gardens
8 Viaduct Gardens, Nine Elms
London SW11 7BW

Ebury Edge is part of the Penguin Random House group of companies
whose addresses can be found at global.penguinrandomhouse.com

Penguin
Random House
UK

First published in Great Britain in 2021 by Ebury Edge
First published in the United States by Currency in 2021
This edition published in Great Britain in 2025 by Ebury Edge

www.penguin.co.uk

A CIP catalogue record for this book is available from the British Library

ISBN 9780753558805

Book illustrations by Greg McKeown and Denisse Leon

Printed and bound in Great Britain by Clays Ltd, Elcograf S.p.A.

The authorised representative in the EEA is Penguin Random House Ireland,
Morrison Chambers, 32 Nassau Street, Dublin D02 YH68

Penguin Random House is committed to a sustainable future
for our business, our readers and our planet. This book is made
from Forest Stewardship Council® certified paper.

FSC
www.fsc.org
MIX
Paper | Supporting responsible forestry
FSC® C018179

For my yoke is easy, and my burden is light.

—Matt. 11:30

CONTENTS

effortless

Introduction

NOT EVERYTHING HAS TO BE SO HARD

Let me tell you the story of Patrick McGinnis.

He had done all the things he was supposed to do. He had checked all the boxes. He'd graduated from Georgetown University. Then from Harvard Business School. He'd joined the ranks of a top finance and insurance company.

He put in the long workdays he felt were expected of him: to the tune of eighty hours per week, even on vacations and holidays. He never left the office before his boss; sometimes it felt as though he never left the office at all.

He traveled so much for work that he earned the highest frequent flier status on Delta, a level so high it didn't even have a name. Meanwhile, he was on the boards of four companies on three continents. Once, when he refused to stay home sick, he had to leave a board meeting three times to throw up in the bathroom. When he returned, a colleague said he looked green. But, still, he powered through.

He had been taught that hard work is the key to everything you want in life. It was a part of the New England mindset: your work ethic was evidence of your character. And, ever the overachiever, he'd taken this to the next level. He didn't just think that working endless hours would lead to success; he thought it *was* success. If you didn't stay late at work, you must not have a very important job.

He assumed that in the end, his long hours would pay off. Then one day he woke up to find himself working for a bankrupt company. That company was AIG and the year was 2008. His stock had fallen 97 percent. All the late nights at the office, all the countless red-eye flights to Europe, South America, and China, all the missed birthdays and celebrations, had been for naught.

In the months after the financial crisis hit, McGinnis couldn't get out of bed. He started having night sweats. His vision blurred, both literally and figuratively. He couldn't see clearly for months. He was floundering. Lost.

He was sick with stress. His doctor ran some tests. He felt like the tragic character Boxer the Horse in George Orwell's *Animal Farm,* described as the farm's most dedicated laborer whose answer to every problem, every setback, was "I will work harder"—that is, until he collapsed from overwork and was sent to the knackers' yard.

So on the cab ride back from the doctor's office McGinnis made what he called "a bargain with God." He promised, "If I survive this, then I will really make some changes."

"Working longer and harder had been the solution to every problem," McGinnis said. But all of a sudden, he realized, "The marginal return of working harder was, in fact, negative."

So what could he do? He had three options. He could carry on and likely work himself to death. He could aim lower and give up on his goals. Or he could find an easier way to achieve the success he wanted.

He chose the third option.

He stepped down from his role at AIG but stayed on as a consultant. He stopped working eighty hours a week. He started going home at five. He no longer emailed on the weekends.

He also stopped treating sleep like a necessary evil. He started walking, running, and eating better. He lost twenty-five pounds. He started enjoying his life, and his work, again.

Around this time, he was inspired by a friend who was investing in start-ups—not a lot of money, just small checks here and there. It piqued Patrick's interest.

He invested in a couple of companies. He has a twenty-five-fold return on his portfolio of investments. Even during tough economic times he's felt sanguine about his finances because he isn't dependent on a single source of income.

He has made more money in half the hours he used to work. And the type of work he is doing is more rewarding, less intrusive. He said, "It doesn't even feel like work anymore."

What he learned from this experience was this: When you simply can't try any harder, it's time to find a different path.

What about you? Do you ever feel as though

- you're running faster but not moving any closer to your goals?
- you want to make a higher contribution but lack the energy?
- you're teetering right on the edge of burnout?
- things are so much harder than they ought to be?

If you answered yes to any or all of these, this book is for you.

These people are disciplined and focused. They are engaged and motivated. And yet, they are utterly exhausted.

The Effortless Way

There is an ebb and flow to life. Rhythms are in everything we do. There are times to push hard and times to rest and recuperate. But these days many of us are pushing harder and harder all the time. There is no cadence, only grinding effort.

We live in a time of great opportunity. But there is something about modern life that's like trying to hike at high altitude. Our brains are foggy. The ground beneath our feet seems unsteady. The air is thin and it can feel surprisingly exhausting to make even an inch of progress. Perhaps it's the endless fear and uncertainty about the future. Perhaps it's the loneliness and isolation. Perhaps it's financial worries or hardships. Perhaps it's all the responsibilities, all the pressures that can suffocate us on a daily basis. Whatever the cause, the result is that we're often working twice as hard only to achieve half as much.

Life is hard, really hard, in all sorts of ways, ranging from the complicated to the weighty, the sad to the exhausting. Disappointments are hard. Paying the bills is hard. Strained relationships are hard. Raising children is hard. Losing a loved one is hard. There are periods in our lives when every day can be hard.

To try to pretend that a book can eliminate these hardships would be fanciful. I didn't write this book to downplay these burdens; I wrote it to help you lighten them. This book may not make every hard thing easy to approach and carry, but I believe it can make many hard things easier.

It's normal to feel overwhelmed and exhausted by the big, weighty challenges. And it's equally normal to feel overwhelmed and exhausted by the everyday frustrations and annoyances. It happens to us all. And these days it seems like it's happening to more of us, more often than it used to.

Strangely, some of us respond to feeling exhausted and overwhelmed by vowing to work even harder and longer. It doesn't help that our culture glorifies burnout as a measure of success and self-worth. The implicit message is that if we aren't perpetually exhausted, we must not be doing enough. That great things are reserved for those who bleed, for those who almost break. Crushing volume is somehow now the goal.

Burnout is not a badge of honor.

It is true that hard work can equal better results. But this is true only to a point. After all, there's an upper limit to how much time and effort we can invest. And the more depleted we get, the more our return on that effort dwindles. This cycle can continue until we are burned out and exhausted, and *still* haven't produced the results we really want. You probably know this. You may be experiencing it right now.

But what if, instead, we took the opposite approach? If instead of pushing ourselves to, and in some cases well past, our limit, we sought out an easier path?

The Dilemma

After my first book, *Essentialism: The Disciplined Pursuit of Less,** was published, I hit the speaking circuit. I had the opportunity to travel the country giving keynotes, signing books, and sharing a message that was close to my heart. My wife, Anna, loved that I often took one of the children with me on these adventures, and so did I. On one such trip, I arrived at my book signing at the scheduled time to find that three hundred people had lined up around the corner and the store had run out of books—which had never happened before at an event. That year was a blur of airport lounges, Ubers, and hotel rooms, to which I would return in the evenings, exhilarated and exhausted, and call down for room service. The success of *Essentialism* had changed everything.

People who had read or listened to the book three, five, or seventeen times wrote to tell me about how the book had changed their life, or in some cases even saved it. Each of them wanted to share their stories with me—and I wanted to hear them.

I wanted to speak in front of rooms full of people who were eager to become Essentialists. I wanted to respond to every email I received from readers. I wanted to write personalized messages to everyone who asked me to sign copies of the book. I wanted to be present and gracious with every person who had a story to tell about their experience with *Essentialism.*

Even better than being the "Father of Essentialism," was being a father, now to four children. My family epitomizes everything that's essential to me, so I wanted to invest in it fully. I wanted to be a true partner to Anna and to make space for her to pursue her own goals and dreams. To really listen to the children whenever they

* I invite you to design a more essential and effortless lifestyle by going to the Essentialism Academy at essentialism.com.

wanted to talk, however inconvenient those times often seemed. I wanted to be there to celebrate their successes. I wanted to coach them and encourage them to achieve whatever goals felt most essential to them, whether that was to direct a movie or become an Eagle Scout. I wanted to play board games together, to wrestle, to swim together, to play tennis, to go to the beach, to do movie night with popcorn and treats.

To make time for such things, I had already stripped away many nonessentials: I'd resisted writing a new book even though I'd been told I was "supposed to" do so every eighteen months. I'd taken a break from teaching my class at Stanford. I'd set aside my plans to build a workshop business.

I'd never been more selective in my life. The problem was, it still felt like too much. And not only that: I felt a call to increase my contribution even while I had run out of space.

I was striving to model Essentialism. To live what I teach. But it wasn't enough. I could feel the cracks in an assumption I had always held to: that to achieve everything we want without becoming impossibly busy or overextended, we simply need to discipline ourselves to only say "yes" to essential activities and "no" to everything else. But now I found myself wondering: what does one do when they've stripped life down to the essentials and it's *still* too much?

Around that time, I was teaching a group of extremely thoughtful entrepreneurs when someone had referenced the "big rocks theory."

It's the well-known story of a teacher who picks up a large empty jar. She pours in some small pebbles at the bottom. Then she tries to place some larger rocks on top. The problem is that they don't fit.

The teacher then gets a new empty container of the same size. This time she puts the large rocks in first. Then the small pebbles in second. This time they fit.

This is, of course, a metaphor. The big rocks represent the most essential responsibilities like health, family, and relationships. The small pebbles are less important things like work and career. The sand are things like social media and doom swiping.

The lesson is similar to the one I'd always ascribed to: if you prioritize the most important things first, then there will be room in your life not only for what matters most but also for other things too. But do the reverse, and you'll get the trivial things done but run out of space for the things that really matter.

But as I sat in my hotel room that night, I wondered: What do you do if there are too many big rocks? What if the absolutely essential work simply does not fit within the limits of the container?

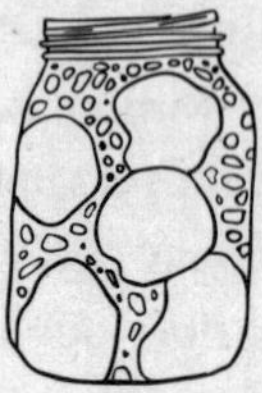

How it's supposed to work

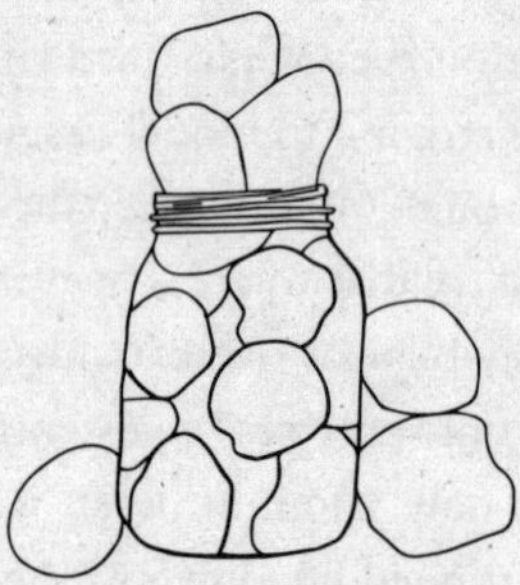

But what if there are too many big rocks?

As I pondered this, I got a video call. It was my son Jack calling from my wife's phone. That was unusual and immediately got my attention. I noticed that his face was drained of its color. His tone was urgent. He looked scared. I could hear my wife's voice in the background instructing Jack to "turn the phone around" so I could see what was going on.

He tried to explain: "Eve . . . something really wrong. . . . She was just eating and then her head started moving. . . . Mom . . . told me to call you."

Eve was having a massive tonic-clonic seizure.

The adrenaline got me through what I did next: hastily packing and taking the red-eye flight back to my family. But what would follow in the days and weeks ahead left me emotionally drained. There were the hospital visits. The consultations with medical experts. The endless phone calls from friends and family who wanted to know how we were holding up and how they could help. Meanwhile, I discovered that all my other responsibilities didn't miraculously disappear just because I was in the middle of a crisis. There were still keynotes to reschedule. Flights to cancel. Essential emails to answer.

The walls closed in around me. I was burdened beyond belief. It was suffocating at times. I wanted to collapse under it all. It was torture.

This went on for many weeks. Eventually, I recognized the situation for what it was: I was burned out. I had literally written the book on how to be an Essentialist, and here I was, overwhelmed and spread far too thin. I felt self-imposed pressure to be the perfect Essentialist, but there were no nonessentials left to eliminate. It all mattered. Finally I said to Anna: "I'm not well."

Here is what I learned: I was doing all the right things for the right reasons. But I was doing them in the wrong way.

I was like a weightlifter trying to lift using the muscles in my lower back. A swimmer who hadn't learned to breathe properly. A baker who was painstakingly kneading each loaf of bread by hand.

I suspect you know exactly what I'm talking about. I'm guessing you know what it's like to feel highly engaged by your work but on the edge of exhaustion. To be doing the best you can but still feel it isn't enough. To have more essentials than you can fit into your day. To want to do more but simply don't have the space. To be making progress on things that matter but too weary to derive any joy from your successes.

For you who gives so much, I say this: there is another way.

Not everything has to be so hard. Getting to the next level doesn't have to mean chronic exhaustion. Making a contribution doesn't have to come at the expense of your mental and physical health.

When the essentials become too hard to handle, you can either give up on them or you can find an easier way.

Essentialism was about doing the right things; *Effortless* is about doing them in the right way.

Since writing *Essentialism*, I have had a rare opportunity to talk with thousands of people, some in person, some via social media, and some of them on my podcast, about the challenges they face in trying to live a life that really matters. It has been a multiyear listening tour. Never in my life have I had an opportunity to listen to so many people sharing, so vulnerably, how they struggle to do what matters most.

What I learned is this: we all want to do what matters. We want to get in shape, save for a home or for retirement, be fulfilled in our careers, and build closer relationships with people we work and live with. The problem isn't a lack of motivation; if it were, we would all already be at our ideal weight, live within our means, have our dream job, and enjoy deep and meaningful relationships with all the people who matter most to us.

Motivation is not enough because it is a limited resource. To truly make progress on the things that matter, we need a whole new way to work and live.

Instead of trying to get better results by pushing ever harder, we can make the most essential activities the easiest ones.

For some, the idea of working less hard feels uncomfortable. We feel lazy. We fear we'll fall behind. We feel guilty for not "going the extra mile" each time. This mindset, conscious or not, may have its roots in the Puritan idea that the act of doing hard things always has an inherent value. Puritanism went beyond embracing the hard; it extended to also distrusting the easy. But achieving our goals efficiently isn't unambitious. It's smart. It's a liberating alternative to both hard work and laziness: one that allows us to preserve our sanity while still accomplishing everything we want.

What could happen in your life if the easy but pointless things became harder and the essential things became easier?

What could happen in your life if the easy but pointless things became harder and the essential things became easier? If the essential projects you've been putting off became enjoyable, while the pointless distractions lost their appeal completely? Such a shift would stack the deck in our favor. It would change everything. It *does* change everything.

That's the value proposition of *Effortless.* It's about a whole new way to work and live. A way to achieve more with ease—to achieve more *because* you are at ease. A way to lighten life's inevitable burdens, and get the right results without burning out.

Nothing but Net

This book is organized into three simple parts:

Part I reintroduces you to your Effortless State.
Part II shows how to take Effortless Action.
Part III is about achieving Effortless Results.

Each of these builds upon the last.

Think of an NBA player stepping up to take a free throw.

First, they get into "the zone." They find the "dot" on the free throw line, dribble the ball a few times: a ritual to help them get completely focused. You can almost see them clearing their heads—letting go of all emotions, blocking out the noise of the crowd. This is what I call the *Effortless State.*

Second, they bend their knees, bring their front elbow to the right angle, and then "lift, flick, and pop." They have practiced this precise, flowing movement until it has sunk deep into their muscle memory. They try without trying, fluid and smooth in their execution. This is *Effortless Action.*

Third, the ball arcs through the air and goes into the basket. It makes that satisfying swish: the sound of a perfectly executed free throw. It's not a fluke. They can do it again and again. This is what it feels like to achieve *Effortless Results.*

Part I: Effortless State

When our brains are at full capacity, everything feels harder. Fatigue slows us down. Outdated assumptions and emotions make new information harder to process. The countless distractions of daily life make it difficult to see what matters clearly.

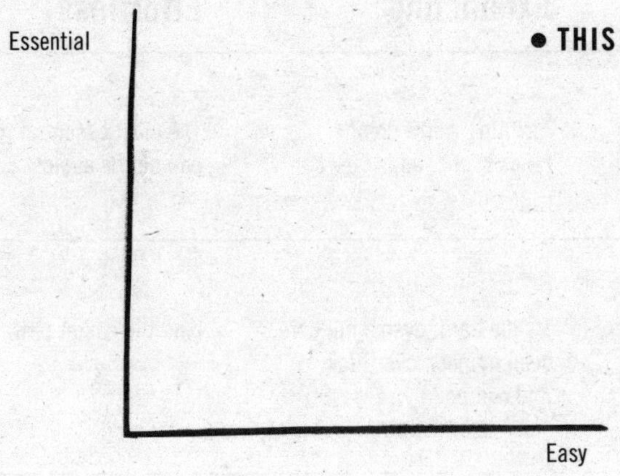

So the first step toward making things more effortless is to clear the clutter in our heads and our hearts.

You have likely experienced this before. It's when you feel rested, at peace, and focused. You're fully present in the moment. You have a heightened awareness of what matters here and now. You feel capable of taking the right action.

This part of the book provides actionable ways to return to the Effortless State.

The Model

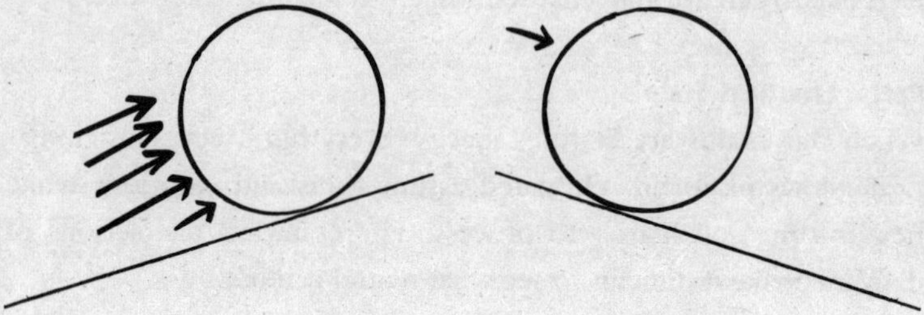

	Exhausting	Effortless
Think	Anything worth doing takes tremendous effort	The most essential things can be the easiest ones
Do	Try too hard: overcomplicate, overengineer, overthink, and overdo	Find the easier path
Get	Burnout and none of the results you want	The right results without burning out

Part II: Effortless Action

Once we are in the Effortless State, it becomes easier to take Effortless Action. But we may still encounter complexity that makes it hard to start or advance an essential project. Perfectionism makes essential projects hard to start, self-doubt makes them hard to finish, and trying to do too much, too fast, makes it hard to sustain momentum.

This part of the book is all about simplifying the process to make the work itself easier to do.

Part III: Effortless Results

When we take Effortless Action, we make it easier to get the results we want.

There are two types of results: linear and residual.

Whenever your efforts yield a one-time benefit, you are getting a *linear result*. Every day you start from zero; if you don't put in the effort today then you don't get the result today. It's a one-to-one ratio; the amount of effort you put in equals the results received. But what if those results could flow to us repeatedly, without further effort on our part?

With *residual results* you put in the effort once and reap the benefits again and again. Results flow to you while you are sleeping. Results flow to you when you are taking the day off. Residual results can be virtually infinite.

Effortless Action alone produces linear results. But when we apply Effortless Action to high-leverage activities, the return on our effort compounds, like interest on a savings account. This is how we produce residual results.

Producing a great result is good. Producing a great result with ease is better. Producing a great result with ease again and again is best. That is what part III of the book shows how to do.

Anything Can Be Made Effortless, but Not Everything

Discovering the effortless way of living is like using special polarized sunglasses while fly-fishing. Without them, the glare on the water makes it difficult to see anything swimming below the surface. But as soon as you put them on, their angled surface filters out the horizontal light waves coming off the water, blocking the glare. Suddenly, you can see all the fish underneath.

When we're accustomed to doing things the hard way, it's like being blinded by the glare coming off the water. But once you start putting these ideas into practice you will start to see that the easier way was there all along, just hidden from your view.

We've all experienced how the effortless way can feel. For example, have you ever

- been in a relaxed state and found it easier to get in "the zone"?
- stopped trying so hard and actually got better results?
- done something once that has benefited you multiple times?

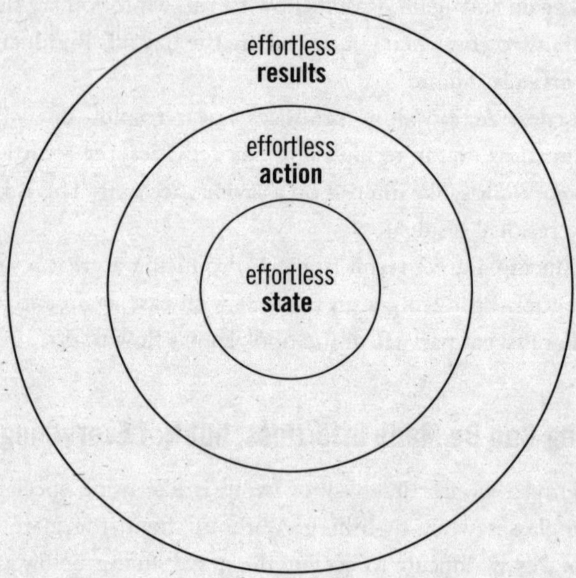

My motivation for writing this book is singular: to help you experience more of this, more of the time.

Of course, you can't make everything in your life effortless. But you can make more of the right things less impossible—then easier, then easy, and ultimately effortless.

In writing this book, I have interviewed experts and read their research, drawing on learnings from behavioral economics, philosophy, psychology, physics, and neuroscience. I made a disciplined pursuit of uncovering answers to the essential question "How can I make it easier to do what matters most?" Now I can't wait to share all that I've learned with you—because, in the words of George Eliot, "What do we live for, if not to make life less difficult for each other?"

effortless state

PART I

The best free throw shooter ever is not Michael Jordan or Steph Curry. It's Elena Delle Donne. Her success rate at the free throw line across her career is 93.4 percent. That's not just the highest in WNBA history but higher than any player in NBA history as well. If you look at her postseason record it's even higher: 96.4 percent. Put simply: she is the best free throw shooter ever.

Her secret is to trust the simple process she has practiced since eighth grade. She steps up to the line, finds the dot with her right foot, lines up her feet, takes three dribbles, makes an L with her arm, then lifts and flicks. "If you keep it simple, less can go wrong," she says.

The most important part of the process? "Not overthinking it. The biggest thing on the foul line is you can't let too much get inside your head."

In other words, the secret to Donne's success is her ability to get into what I call the *Effortless State*.

You are like a supercomputer designed with extremely powerful capabilities. You're built to be able to learn quickly, solve problems intuitively, and compute the right next action effortlessly.

Under optimal conditions, your brain works at incredible speeds. But just like a supercomputer, your brain does not always perform optimally. Think about how a computer slows down when its hard drive gets cluttered with files and browsing data. The machine still has incredible computing power, but it's less available to perform essential functions. Similarly, when your brain is filled with clutter—like outdated assumptions, negative emotions, and toxic thought patterns—you have less mental energy available to perform what's most essential.

A concept in cognitive psychology known as perceptual load theory explains why this is the case. Our brain's processing capacity is large, but limited. It already processes over six thousand thoughts a day. So when we encounter new information, our brains have to make a choice about how to allocate the remaining cognitive resources. And because our brains are programmed to prioritize emotions with high "affective value"—like fear, resentment, or anger—these strong emotions will generally win out, leaving us with even fewer mental resources to devote to making progress on the things that matter.

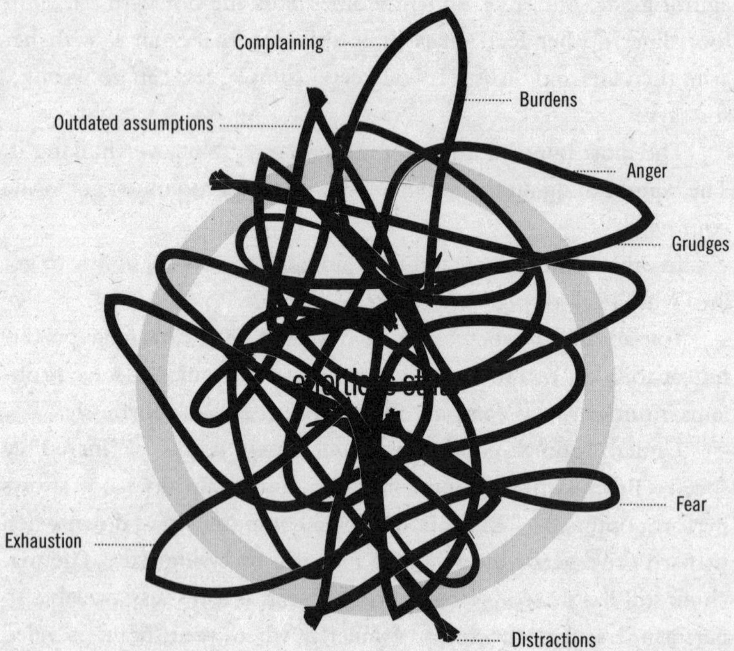

effortless state

When your computer is running slowly, all you have to do is hit a few buttons to clear all the browsing data, and immediately the machine works smoother and faster. In a similar way, you can learn simple tactics to rid yourself of all the clutter slowing down the hard drive of your mind. By hitting a few buttons, you can be restored to your original Effortless State.

Perhaps you have experienced what it feels like to return to the Effortless State. Imagine it's the end of a long day. You have a headache that you can't seem to shake. You can't remember where you've put your phone. Or your keys. Even the smallest, most reasonable requests—a client asks for a piece of information via a confusing voicemail, or your child wants to be picked up from piano lessons—fill you with resentment. A piece of constructive feedback from your boss spins you out—you're convinced you're a failure. You're irritable with your spouse, and can't find the right words to express how overwhelmed you feel. Why does *everything* feel so hard? you wonder.

Then, after a warm meal, a hot shower, and a good night's sleep, things look completely different. You wake up clearheaded, grateful for another day. You find your phone and your keys (right where you left them!). You immediately know how to respond to the voicemail (not so confusing after all!), and you do so with grace. You want nothing more than to sit quietly in the car with your child for a few minutes on the way back from piano lessons. You find the right words to say to your spouse: "I'm sorry about that! Please forgive me." You thank your boss for the feedback and mean it. Your inherent capabilities are restored.

When you return to your Effortless State, *you feel lighter*, in the two senses of the word. First, you feel less heavy—unburdened. You aren't as weighed down. Suddenly you have more energy.

But *lighter* also means more full of light. When you remove the burdens in your heart and the distractions in your mind, you are able to see more clearly. You can discern the right action and light the right path.

The Effortless State is one in which you are physically rested, emotionally unburdened, and mentally energized. You are completely present, attentive, and focused on what's important in that moment. You are able to do what matters most with ease.

CHAPTER 1

INVERT

What If This Could Be Easy?

"Four A.M. and I'm up photoshopping pictures? Really?"

Kim Jenkins wanted to do what really mattered. But it was hard not to feel overwhelmed. For one thing, the university where she worked was undergoing an immense expansion. The client base had doubled in the last few years, but they were operating with virtually the same staff and resources as before.

With the expansion of the organization had come an expansion of complexity everywhere. There were new and difficult-to-decipher internal policies. There was a tedious new system for handling compliance. Processes had grown cumbersome, and now all of their projects and programs took more energy and time. Well-intentioned people had added but never subtracted. They had taken work that used to be simple and made it maddeningly, unnecessarily complicated.

As a result, the effort required to get her work done had become Herculean. And Kim had a tendency to be really hard on herself.

She said, "I thought if I wasn't putting in tremendous effort, sacrificing any time for myself, then I was being incredibly selfish."

Then one day, it hit her. This was all so much *harder* than it ought to be. And with that realization, she said, "I could see it all for what it was: layers and layers of unnecessary complexity. I could see how it was expanding all the time and how I was suffocating underneath all of it."

She decided it was time to make a change: When faced with a task that felt impossibly hard, she would ask, "Is there an easier way?"

She soon had the opportunity to put this method to the test when a faculty member called her and asked if she could have her videography team record a full semester of a class. In the past she would have jumped in with both feet, put her team to work for four months, and looked for ways to go above and beyond: adding music, intros and outros, and graphics. This time she wondered if there was an easier way to get the desired results. A brief conversation revealed that the videos were intended for a single student who couldn't make every class due to a sports commitment. He didn't need a highly produced recording with lots of bells and whistles; he just needed a way to avoid falling behind in his class. So she thought, "What if they simply asked another student to record those lectures on a smartphone?" "The professor was delighted with the solution," Kim said. And it cost her just a couple of minutes of planning instead of months of work for her whole videography team.

Hard Work May Not Be Well Named

All too often, we sacrifice our time, our energy, and even our sanity, almost believing that sacrifice is essential in and of itself. The problem is that the complexity of modern life has created a false dichotomy between things that are "essential and hard" and things that are "easy and trivial." It's almost like a natural law for some people: Trivial things are easy. Important things are hard.

Our language helps to reveal our deeper assumptions. Think of these revealing phrases: When we accomplish something important, we say it took "blood, sweat, and tears." We say important achievements are "hard-earned" when we might just say "earned." We recommend a "hard day's work" when "day's work" would suffice.

Then there are the ways our language betrays our distrust of ease. When we talk of "easy money," we are implying it was obtained through illegal or questionable means. We use the phrase "That's easy for you to say" as a criticism, usually when we are seeking to invalidate someone's opinion.

It's curious to me how we default to sayings like "It won't be easy, but it's worth it" or "It's going to be really hard to make that happen, but we should try." It's like we all automatically accept that the "right" way is, inevitably, the harder one.

In my experience this is hardly ever questioned. Indeed, if you do challenge this sacred cow, it can be uncomfortable. We don't even pause to consider that something important and valuable could be made easy.

What if the biggest thing keeping us from doing what matters is the false assumption that it has to take tremendous effort? What if, instead, we considered the possibility that the reason something feels hard is that we haven't yet found the easier way to do it?

The Path of Least Effort

Our brain is wired to resist what it perceives as hard and welcome what it perceives as easy.

This bias is sometimes called the *cognitive ease principle,* or the *principle of least effort.* It's our tendency to take the path of least resistance to achieve what we want.

We don't need to look far to see the principle in action. We buy something at the overpriced convenience store on the corner because it's easier than getting in the car and driving to the store where prices are lower. We put our dishes in the sink instead of the dishwasher because one less step is required. We let our teenager text through dinner because it's easier than inviting an argument by trying to enforce the no-phones rule. We accept the first, minimally credible information we find online about a subject because it's the easiest way to get our questions answered. And so on.

From an evolutionary perspective, this bias for ease is useful. For most of human history it's been crucial to our survival and progress. Just imagine if humans had a bias for the path of *most* resistance. What if our ancestors had been wired to ask, "What's the hardest way to obtain food? To provide our family shelter? To maintain relationships within our tribe?" They wouldn't have made it! Our survival as a species grows out of innate preference for taking the path of least effort.

What if, rather than fighting our preprogrammed instinct to seek the easiest path, we could embrace it, even use it to our advantage? What if, instead of asking, "How can I tackle this really hard but essential project?," we simply inverted the question and asked, "What if this essential project could be made easy?"

For some, the idea of working less hard feels uncomfortable. We feel lazy. We fear we'll fall behind. We feel guilty for not "going the extra mile" each time. This mindset, conscious or not, may have its roots in the Puritan idea that the act of doing hard things always has an inherent value. Puritanism went beyond embracing the hard; it extended to also distrusting the easy.

How to Try Too Hard

At a key moment in my career, a client at a high-profile technology company asked me to give three presentations on leadership. They told me that if all went well they were prepared to hire me for the next year or more. It was exactly the career break I needed. I understood their needs well. I had ready-made content they had already approved.

The afternoon before the first presentation, I decided to add some finishing touches. It already looked good. But I worried it didn't look good *enough*. I decided to scrap it all and start over.

I got consumed with a new idea that I was convinced would wow them. I ended up staying up all night rewriting my whole presentation: new slides, new handouts, all of which were, of course, untested.

As I drove to the company's offices the next morning I was exhausted. My mind was foggy. When I arrived, I was running on the fumes of my nervous energy.

As the presentation began, my stomach sank. My opening story was unpolished. The slides were unfamiliar; I kept having to turn around to see what was on the screen. One of the first slides failed to convey the point I was trying to make.

In short, I bombed. As I left, I was hyperventilating. I had been given this incredible opportunity, and I had blown it.

The client canceled the other two presentations. They did not hire me for the extended engagement. It was my most humiliating professional failure—ever.

I was burned-out from the experience, *and* I didn't even walk away with the results I wanted.

As I reflected on how this had all gone so wrong, the answer was obvious. Nailing this presentation was so important to me, I had overthought it. I'd overengineered it. I'd tried too hard. And as a result, I'd snatched defeat from the jaws of victory.

Here is what I learned: trying too hard makes it harder to get the results you want.

Here is what I realized: behind almost every failure of my whole life I had made the same error. When I'd failed, it was rarely because I hadn't tried hard enough, it was because I'd been trying too hard.

We are conditioned over the course of our lifetimes to believe that in order to overachieve we must also overdo. As a result, we make things harder for ourselves than they need to be.

Effortless Inversion

Carl Jacobi, the nineteenth-century German mathematician, developed a reputation as someone who could solve especially hard and intractable problems. He learned that to do that most easily, *Man muss immer umkehren,* which translates to "One must invert, always invert."

To invert means to turn an assumption or approach upside down, to work backward, to ask, "What if the opposite were true?" Inversion can help you discover obvious insights you have missed because you're looking at the problem from only one point of view. It can highlight errors in our thinking. It can open our minds to new ways of doing things.

Assuming that all worthwhile things take enormous effort is one way of looking at a problem. For many overachievers it's the only way. They have learned how to solve problems even when exhausted or overwhelmed. They are good at getting things done by powering through.

Effortless Inversion means looking at problems from the opposite perspective. It means asking, "What if this could be easy?" It means learning to solve problems from a state of focus, clarity, and calm. It means getting good at getting things done by putting in *less* effort.

There are two ways to achieve all the things that really matter. We can (a) gain superhuman powers so we can do all the impossibly hard but worthwhile work or (b) get better at making the impossibly hard but worthwhile work easier.

Once we invert the question, even everyday tasks that seem too overwhelming to tackle become easier.

For example, the other day I was tidying up my office. As I scanned the room I saw an old printer we had recently replaced. It had been sitting on my office floor for a couple of weeks, taking up space. It bothered me every time I saw it there. Still, every time I looked at it I thought of all the steps required to deal with it: deciding whether to keep or discard it, checking the costs of replacing the color ink, potentially finding a place to give it away. Every time, the work involved was enough for a voice in my head to whisper, "Too much trouble!" so I quickly resigned myself to it staying on the floor.

However, this time I asked, "What if this could be easy?" What if all those steps I'd assumed this task entailed were not in fact required steps at all? I then looked up from my desk and happened to see one of the building workers through the window of my office. I walked outside and asked if he wanted the printer for free. He said yes, and took it. The problem was solved within two minutes of asking the question.

When we feel overwhelmed, it may not be because the situation is inherently overwhelming. It may be because we are overcomplicating something in our own heads. Asking the question "What if this could be easy?" is a way to reset our thinking. It may seem almost impossibly simple. And that's exactly why it works.

Weaken the Impossible

The abolitionist William Wilberforce approached his impossibly hard, worthwhile work with great conviction. As a member of Parliament in Britain at the beginning of the nineteenth century, he fought for the moral case against slavery. He rallied his generation to do the same. He wanted to attack the slave trade with sweeping legislation to end this barbaric and inhumane system.

But for all his effort, and for all his fervor, he couldn't make a dent in the law. The forces working against him were massive. There were powerful parties intent on protecting the status quo. There were bystanders who were too consumed with other things to care. There were others who cared, but not enough to make the necessary sacrifices. The barriers were too great, the interests too entrenched, the distractions too many.

Then one of his fellow abolitionists, James Stephen, had an idea. Rather than continuing to attack the system head-on, he suggested a more indirect approach.

In 1805, Stephen wrote a pamphlet entitled *War in Disguise; or, The Frauds of the Neutral Flags.* In it he argued against the use by warring nations of neutral flags on ships. At a time when France and England were at war, French cargo ships were sailing under the neutral American flag to take advantage of maritime law that protected them from seizure by the enemy. The majority of slave ships sailing to the West Indies were also flying the American flag because, under the law at the time, this meant they could not be stopped by the British Navy.

Stephen saw that if England were to change the law to remove that protection, no slave trader would dare allow his vessel to make the journey. Without the protection of neutral flags, the bulk of the British slave trade would be eliminated.

Fearing that if he mentioned the slave trade his arguments

might be dismissed, Stephen confined himself entirely to issues of war. His outwardly uncontroversial treatise was swiftly published and went largely unopposed.

This seemingly innocuous, deliberately dull paper was in reality a Trojan horse. Beginning in January 1807, the British Privy Council issued the first of a series of war measures against Napoleon, inspired by Stephen's approach. The effect was as had been hoped for. While there were still many battles left to be fought in the name of abolition and racial justice (and still are today), the unconscionable practice of trading enslaved people was formally outlawed across the British Empire just two months later, with the passing of the Abolition of the Slave Trade Act.

There's no question that some goals are incredibly, almost impossibly, hard to achieve. However, even these can sometimes be made less hard, once we find an indirect approach.

A One-Way Ticket to Easy

Southwest Airlines did just that when they faced a different kind of crisis. Ever since the airline's founding, its business model had depended on keeping costs low and turning planes around on a dime after they'd landed. Both of these goals were incompatible with the traditional system for printing out tickets. Passengers were accustomed to the industry standard of being handed a printed ticket when they checked in for their flight, but because of the reservation system technology available at the time, producing paper tickets for each passenger was expensive, and they took too long to print at the gate. So executives were forced to decide whether to pay $2 million to build a modern ticketing system.

The case for creating the new system was compelling: if we don't do it, management thought, we risk going out of business. But $2 million was a major hit to the bottom line for a low-cost carrier, especially for something that served no practical purpose other than to conform to the practices of the industry.

Southwest cofounder Herb Kelleher insisted there had to be a better way: "We are sitting in a management meeting trying to figure out what to do," he recalls, "when someone piped up and asked 'Do we really give a damn what United thinks a ticket is? Isn't it more important what *we* think a ticket is?' Reflexively, we all said, 'No, we only care what we think a ticket is.' So then the manager says, 'Then why don't we just print out a single piece of paper that says 'This is a Ticket.' "

And that's what they did. Instead of wasting time and resources on building an expensive ticketing system, Southwest decided to issue "tickets" that could be printed out on ordinary paper and obtained from no-frills automatic dispensers. Merely questioning the necessity of the complex features and functions of an expensive ticketing system revealed a far simpler, cheaper, and easy-to-execute solution.

Free of the assumptions that make your problem look hard, you would be surprised how often an easier solution appears.

Can You Push Something Downhill?

Marketing author Seth Godin once shared the following: "If you can think about how hard it is to push a business uphill, particularly when you're just getting started, one answer is to say: 'Why don't you just start a different business you can push downhill?' "

Reid Hoffman, the cofounder of LinkedIn, has said, "I have come to learn that part of the business strategy is to solve the simplest, easiest, and most valuable problem. And actually, in fact, part of doing strategy is to solve the easiest problem."

We think that to be extraordinarily successful we have to do the

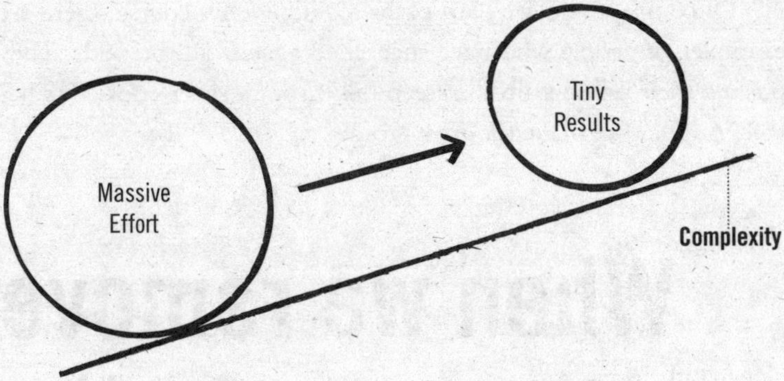

things that are hard and complicated. Instead, we can look for opportunities that are highly valuable *and* simple and easy.

Arianna Huffington used to buy into the notion that anything worth doing required superhuman effort. But she has since said that she didn't become truly successful until she stopped overworking herself. "It's also our collective delusion that overwork and burnout are the price we must pay in order to succeed," she says.

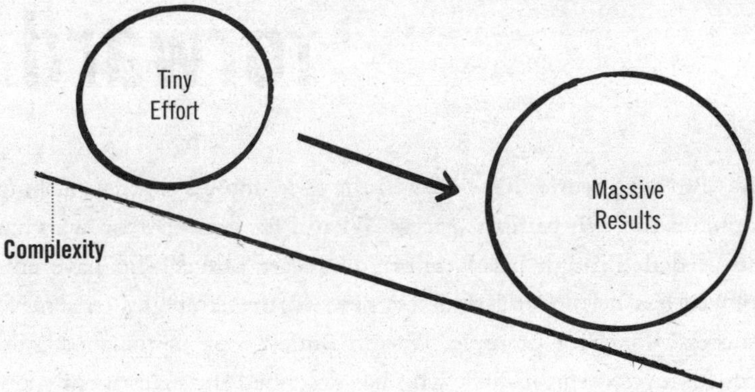

Of course, there are hard paths to success. Of course, there are examples of people who have succeeded against all the odds. They pushed their boulder up the steep hill through sheer effort. It's heroic. And heroes make for great stories.

When we remove the complexity, even the slightest effort can move what matters forward.

But such stories have created the false impression that pushing uphill is the *only* path to success. What if for every person who has succeeded through heroic effort, there are others who have employed less heroic, and thus less newsworthy, strategies to achieve success? Take, for example, Warren Buffett, one of the most successful investors in history, who has described the investment strategy at Berkshire Hathaway as "lethargy bordering on sloth." They are not looking to invest in companies that will require enormous effort to achieve profitability. They are looking for investments that are easy to say yes to: no-brainer businesses that are simple to run and have long-term competitive advantages. In Buffett's words, "I don't look to jump over 7-foot bars: I look around for 1-foot bars that I can step over."

When a strategy is so complex that each step feels akin to pushing a boulder up a hill, you should pause. Invert the problem. Ask, "What's the simplest way to achieve this result?"

In the illustration at the bottom of page 37, we see that when we remove the complexity, even the slightest effort can move what matters forward. Momentum grows with the force of gravity. Execution becomes more effortless.

When we shelve the false assumption that the easier path has to be the inferior path, obstacles fade away. And as these obstacles disappear, we can begin to uncover our Effortless State.

Chapter 2

ENJOY

What If This Could Be Fun?

In 1981, the British activist Jane Tewson was pronounced dead in a refugee camp in Sudan. She had contracted both cerebral malaria and viral pneumonia. There were no drugs left to treat her. She recalls looking down at her own body and then returning to it. Her out-of-body experience proved to be a rebirth, in more ways than one.

Tewson returned to the UK determined to do something about the suffering she had seen firsthand. She knew that to have a real impact she would need to get a lot of people involved. But she also knew the challenge charities face when trying to change people's perceptions, build support, and ultimately raise money. She knew that people *want* to do the right thing and contribute, but, as Gillian Welch wrote, "I want to do right but not right now." She also recognized that asking others for contributions can be like pulling teeth: drudgery for those asking and for the people being asked.

Suddenly Tewson had an idea—one that would affect the lives

of millions of people. If she could make charitable giving "active, emotional, involving and fun," she thought, perhaps it could ease the whole interaction.

Her idea was to pair something people already liked to do—in this case, watch comedy on TV—with contributing to the plight of people in need. The charity was called, brilliantly, Comic Relief.

Comic Relief is best known for Red Nose Days, the first of which took place in February 1988. By this point Tewson had built partnerships with many comedians and celebrities. She reached out to the comedian Lenny Henry, a household name in the UK, and he agreed to become the face of the event. On Christmas Day, Henry announced the launch of the first Red Nose Day from a refugee camp in Safawa.

More than 150 celebrities and comedians participated. The televised event attracted thirty million viewers: more than half the country. People in every corner of the country bought red clown noses, with the proceeds going to the charity. It raised £15 million in a single day. And it's since become a biannual ritual that, over the next thirty years, managed to raise £1 billion for the most disadvantaged people in Africa and for depressed areas within the UK.

Giving to charity is important. Participating in a day of comedy is enjoyable. By bringing charity and comedy together, Tewson made giving easier. As a result, not only do more people participate, they actually *look forward* to participating again, year after year.

We all have things we do consistently not because they are important but because we actively look forward to doing them. Maybe it's listening to a particular podcast, watching a favorite TV show, singing karaoke, dancing to our favorite tunes, or playing games with friends.

At the same time, we all have important activities we *don't* do consistently because we actively dread doing them. Maybe it's exercising, doing our finances, washing the dishes after dinner, returning emails or voicemails, attending meetings, or waking up our teenagers for school. Not every essential activity is inherently enjoyable. But we can make them so.

Why would we simply endure essential activities when we can enjoy them instead?

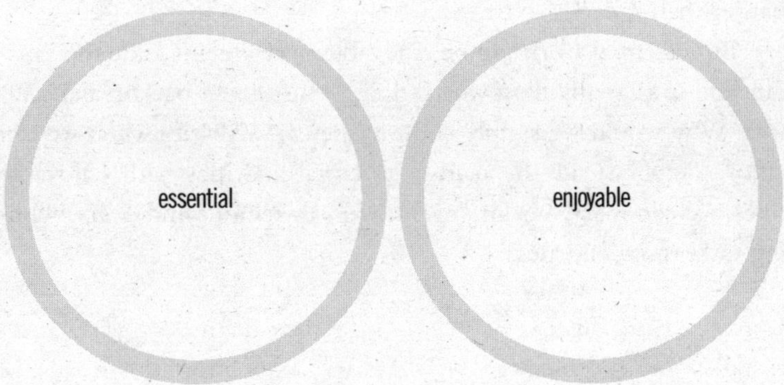

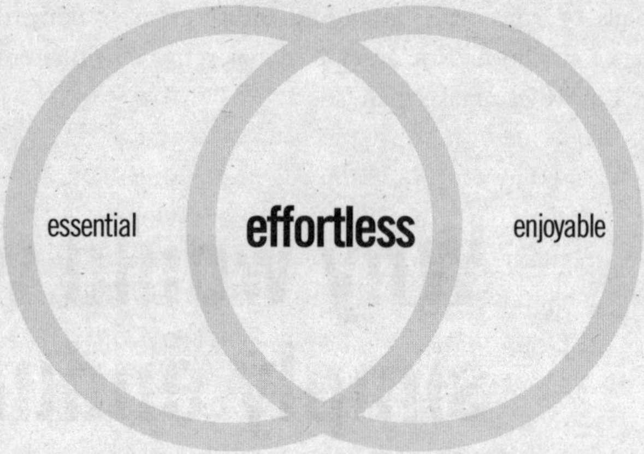

So often we separate important work from trivial play. People say, "I work hard *and then* I can play hard." For many people there are essential things and then there are enjoyable things. But this false dichotomy works against us in two ways. Believing essential activities are, almost by definition, tedious, we are more likely to put them off or avoid them completely. At the same time, our nagging guilt about all the essential work we could be doing instead sucks all the joy out of otherwise enjoyable experiences. Fun becomes "the dark playground." Separating important work from play makes life harder than it needs to be.

But essential work *can* be enjoyable once we put aside the Puritan notion that anything worth doing must entail backbreaking effort. Why would we simply endure essential activities when we can enjoy them instead? By pairing essential activities with enjoyable ones, we can make tackling even the most tedious and overwhelming tasks more effortless.

Reduce the Lag Indicator

It's no secret that many essential activities that are not particularly joyful in the moment produce moments of joy later on. If you exercise and eat better, you will eventually be healthier and lose weight. If you read every day, you will eventually develop expertise. If you meditate regularly, you will eventually develop a greater sense of calm in your life. But these are all lag indicators—meaning, you experience the reward *after* the action has taken place, sometimes weeks, months, or years afterward.

But essential activities don't have to be enjoyed only in retrospect. We can also experience joy in the activity itself. We simply reduce the lag time between the action and satisfaction by pairing the essential activity with a reward.

Once, after a week of travel, I came home to find a backlog of voicemails to respond to. This task initially felt arduous and burdensome. My first thought was "Why do I have so many messages?"—which indicates that I must have been a bit burned-out. But then I realized I was asking the wrong question. So instead I asked, "How can I make calling these people back enjoyable?" After just a few seconds the idea came to make the calls from my hot tub. That changed the whole experience. It put me in a good mood. I told each person that I was calling from the hot tub, and they laughed about it. When I'd finished calling everyone back I almost felt disappointed. I wished I had more people to call.

Ron Culberson is good at many things. He's an accomplished speaker, author, and humorist. In fact, there are few things he does not excel at. But with the Pinewood Derby, he finally met his match.

The Pinewood Derby is a racing event for unpowered, unmanned, miniature cars, run by Cub Scout chapters across the United States. As Culberson describes it, it's "a competition where little boys who are too young to use knives or saws are given a block of wood so that their parents can carve a race car to compete against the other parents' cars. And make no mistake about it, this is a highly competitive event. There are websites where people charge lots of money to sell you the 'secret' of a winning Pinewood Derby car."

Of course, when Culberson's young Cub Scout son asked him to build the fastest car to win the Derby, he agreed. There was one problem: it required a skill that Culberson doesn't possess—craftsmanship.

Being the good dad that he is, Culberson did his best to put together a functioning car. It was a slog, but he pushed through it. Then came race day. They finished last.

But his son would not be deterred, and the following year he asked his father once again to build him a fast car. Culberson groaned on the inside but again did his best. This time, they finished next to last. Meanwhile his son was getting discouraged and Culberson had begun to loathe the entire process.

So when year three rolled around, they took a different approach. Father and son agreed to forgo speed for style: this year, their goal would be to win the Design Award instead of the Speed Award.

This changed everything. Culberson disliked the process of trying to build a fast car because he wasn't good at it. "The whole experience became one design mistake after another. Each car was a disastrous mess of chipped corners, broken axles, and glue," he recalls. "When we went for style, however, I got a second wind. I was able to tap into my humor skills to come up with a funny, creative design that required very little craftsmanship."

That year they designed a car to look like an ice cream sandwich, delivered in an ice cream sandwich box. It was extraordinarily creative, and the talk of the event—but to them, the work had felt effortless. And although they didn't walk away with the Style

Award, they no longer cared; the joy of the experience was enough of a reward in and of itself. "There are many experiences in our work and personal life that are boring, mundane, or even stressful. We often feel that we have no options but to endure them or avoid them," Culberson says. But "if we can break down the processes into those steps, we may find ways to make the steps more bearable, or better yet, fun."

There is power in pairing our most enjoyable activities with our most essential ones. After all, you're probably going to do the enjoyable things anyway. You're going to watch your favorite show, or listen to the new audiobook you just discovered, or relax in your hot tub at some point. So why not pair it with running on the treadmill or doing the dishes or returning phone calls? Perhaps that seems obvious. But how long have you tried to force yourself to do the important but difficult thing through sheer determination, instead of making it fun?

One leader I have worked with sees running on a treadmill every day as an essential habit. Yet he was inconsistent about it until he paired it with an enjoyable daily practice he never missed: listening to his favorite daily podcast. Now he gets to listen to the podcast only if he is walking or running on the treadmill. He doesn't reward himself after he has finished his workout; he rewards himself *during*. Ever since he made this essential practice enjoyable, he has found it easy to continue doing it consistently.

Work Easy, Play Easy

As a family, we eat together every night. It's an essential ritual for us. We make it enjoyable by starting the meal with toasts, praising one another for the accomplishments of the day and expressing what we are thankful for.

After dinner is when it all starts to break down.

When it's time to clear the dinner table and clean up the kitchen it is amazing to see how quickly—and how stealthily—our children disappear. They are like ninjas: silently slipping away to their bedrooms without the slightest sound or disturbance. Then comes the unenviable job of calling them back, one by one, to do the cleanup work. It feels less like parenting and more like a game of cat and mouse. The excuses, "I need to go to the bathroom" or "I have homework," are frustratingly hard to argue with. It's exhausting, and our children obviously don't care for it either. They feel bossed around, and they're frustrated with the whole thing too. This is necessary work, but it's unenjoyable for everyone involved. So we decided to approach it in a different way.

We reimagined it as a game. Together, we created a scoreboard: every person was assigned clear responsibilities (like wiping down all of the surfaces or sweeping the floor). For each one completed, they would earn a point. After a few practice rounds, it was "game on." And here's what happened: nothing.

Dinner was over, and the children, once again, were mysteriously gone. The ninjas were back in full effect.

It wasn't until my eldest daughter added a new ingredient that everything changed. She put on a playlist of Disney classics—the kinds of songs that make you want to sing along. And we played them loud. It turned the whole thing into a karaoke party.

We now do this regularly. And no matter how grumpy we might feel on any given day, it's impossible not to get pulled in. Now, if you were to drop in on us after dinner, you'd find us belting out "Let It Go" from *Frozen,* dancing to "I Just Can't Wait to Be King" from *The Lion King,* laughing through "I'll Make a Man Out of You" from *Mulan*. It looks like the famous scene where Tom Cruise and Bryan Brown make drinks together in the movie *Cocktail*. We are sweeping, wiping, washing, drying, and putting away dishes, and all the while we're laughing, dancing, and singing.

Don't underestimate the power of the right soundtrack to ditch the drudgery and get into a groove.

Create Building Blocks of Joy

It's not just that work and play can co-exist, it's that they can complement each other. Together they make it easier to tap into our creativity and come up with novel ideas and solutions. Take Ole Kirk Christiansen, who had the idea to turn his struggling carpentry business into a toy company while tinkering in his empty warehouse. He called his company LEGO, from the danish term *leg godt*, which means "play well."

When the Second World War disrupted the toy business, instead of giving up and shuttering his factories, he stayed curious as plastics entered mass production, eventually creating LEGO's first "Automatic Binding Brick," a breakthrough that led to a whole new suite of products. Later, Christiansen and his team invited children to their offices and in watching them play were inspired to develop entire "play systems"—towns complete with people, buildings, roads, and cars—which exponentially increased their business.

Even to this day, LEGO's offices bustle with activity and joy. And this culture of productive play continues to fuel their creativity, spawning everything from LEGOLAND theme parks around the world, to video games, to TV shows and blockbuster LEGO movies. In 2015 LEGO was named the "world's most powerful brand." It's also a powerful example of how "playing hard" can make hard work feel effortless.

In the same way that LEGO created Automatic Binding Bricks—designed to be stacked and attached in all sorts of combinations—you too can stack and combine your most essential and most joyful activities to construct new effortless experiences.

Anna and I once made our own list of twenty building blocks

of joy and shared them with each other. They included "tidying up a room, or drawer or cupboard that was a mess (i.e., creating order from chaos)," "listening to a particular song, on repeat, again and again," and "eating dark chocolate covered almonds." These lists were easy to create. And once we had them it became even easier to create signature experiences that were essential and enjoyable.

We started with something that was vitally important but also complete drudgery: our weekly financial meeting. I say "weekly," but in reality it was far less frequent, as it was something I often put off in favor of almost any other activity. I knew that once we endured it, there would be a payoff: the feeling that we had our finances in order. But because the reward happened after the fact, it was easy to put off the meeting. So we often did.

Armed with our building blocks of joy, we decided to build a new experience we'd look forward to: We got out the dark-chocolate-covered almonds. We put on "Feeling Good" by Michael Bublé in the background (on repeat). We treated it more like a date than a mundane obligation. That was when I noticed an element of the meeting I'd previously overlooked: the whole exercise involved tidying up a messy area, the family finances! Just noticing that creating order out of chaos was a part of the experience gave me a tangible and immediate benefit.

We turned a task we had in the past barely endured into a ritual we looked forward to.

Create Habits with a Soul

Much has been written on habits. Less has been written about rituals. These terms are sometimes used interchangeably. But behavioral economists insist they are not the same thing at all.

Rituals are similar to habits in the sense that "when I do X, I also do Y." But they are different from habits because of one key component: the psychological satisfaction you experience *when* you do them. Habits explain "what" you do, but rituals are about "how" you do it.

Rituals make essential habits easier to sustain by infusing the habits with meaning. For example, think of Marie Kondo's approach to tidying up. She doesn't simply invite us to get rid of the things cluttering our closets, she suggests a ritual for letting go. We are to thank the item we are discarding. We are to think about the ways in which items create joy.

She writes, "The act of folding is far more than making clothes compact for storage. It is an act of caring, an expression of love and appreciation for the way these clothes support your lifestyle. Therefore, when we fold, we should put our heart into it, thanking our clothes for protecting our bodies."

What is life-changing here is that the reward goes beyond just being relieved to finally have your clothes folded. It's not just something you're happy to have out of the way. The ritual becomes meaningful in and of itself.

Some rituals have meaning beyond what can be fully appreciated by the outside observer. Like how Agatha Christie wrote her best mysteries while eating apples in the bath. How when Beethoven prepared his coffee each morning, he would count, one by one, exactly sixty beans for his cup. How the ancient Romans in the time of Caesar, prone to devise a ritual for almost every aspect of daily life, made a religious ceremony of their first shave—the *depositio barbae*. No matter how silly these behaviors may seem on the surface, doing them consistently can ground us, sooth our anxieties, and return us to an Effortless State in ways that are often understandable only to us.

Our rituals are habits we have put our thumbprint on. Our rituals are habits with a soul.

They have the power to transform a tedious task into an experience that creates joy.

When we invite joy into our daily routine, we are no longer yearning for the far-off day when it might arrive. That day is always today. When we attach small fragments of wonder to mundane tasks, we are no longer waiting for the time when we can finally allow ourselves to relax. That time is always now. As fun and laughs lighten more of our moments, we are drawn back further toward our natural, playful Effortless State.

Chapter 3

RELEASE

The Power of Letting Go

I was staring back at myself in a mirror. Fully dressed in an authentic Stormtrooper costume.

The moment was the culmination of a decades-long dream I had harbored ever since one of my older brothers planted an idea in my six-year-old mind: "Wouldn't it be *so* cool to own a real Stormtrooper costume like they have in the movies?"

The combination of the hype around the *Return of the Jedi* release, along with the instant appeal of any suggestion coming from an older sibling, burned this idea into my mind. It resided there quietly, unquestioned, until I was standing in the store thirty years later looking at myself costumed from head to toe.

In that moment I clearly saw that not one part of me actually wanted to own a Stormtrooper costume. The idea had been added as a "to-do" in my brain three decades before, then had slipped beneath my consciousness. Evidently, it had been in my head all this time, taking up mental space.

Do you have any items like this, living rent-free in your mind? Outdated goals, suggestions, or ideas that snuck into your brain long ago and took up permanent residence? Mindsets that have outlived their usefulness but have been part of you for so long, you barely even notice them?

Anna now uses a shorthand phrase with me to describe this experience. When I think of acting on some suggestion without giving it the proper consideration, she will ask me, "Is this a Stormtrooper?"

Stormtroopers take many forms: regrets that continue to haunt us, grudges we can't seem to let go of, expectations that were realistic at some point but are now getting in our way.

These intruders are like unnecessary applications running in the background of your computer, slowing down all its other functionality. At first they might not seem to affect your speed and agility. But as they keep accumulating, one after another, eventually your operating system starts to run slower. You forget the name of someone you just met. You read and reread the same paragraph without comprehending it. Your brain hurts trying to make simple decisions like what groceries to buy at the store. Tiny mistakes expand their footprint in your brain and start seeming like huge failures. To reclaim that space in your brain, you need to send these Stormtroopers packing.

Focus on What You Have

The French author Guy de Maupassant tells the story of one Maître Hauchecorne, an industrious man who strove to be an upstanding member of his community—that is, until he was falsely accused of an act he did not commit. His supposed crime was picking up someone's lost wallet off the sidewalk (in fact, it was a piece of string) and failing to return it. He was innocent, but the rumor spread from neighbor to neighbor, and soon people in the town where he lived started to judge him harshly. They began treating him differently. In short, they ostracized him.

He could have let the matter go. He could have forgiven his accusers for refusing to hear his side of the story. He could have quietly allowed for their error, taken solace in the fact that his conscience was clear. And, in doing so, he could have gone on to be useful and industrious in service of his community as he had originally intended.

However, he couldn't let go of it. He obsessed about it. He became ill over it. It consumed him, weakened him, and ultimately killed him. His heart was so full of anger and indignation at this injustice, there was no room for forgiveness. Even on his deathbed, delirious and fatigued, he was heard to mutter bitterly, "A little piece of string. A little piece of string."

When we fall victim to misfortune, it's hard not to obsess, lament, or complain about all that we have lost. In fact, complaining is one of the easiest things to do. It's so easy many of us do it incessantly: when someone is late to meet us, when our neighbors are too loud, when there are no parking spaces on the one day we are running late, when we watch the news, and so on.

We live in a complaint culture that gets high on expressing outrage: especially on social media, which often seems like an endless stream of grumbling and whining about what is unsatisfactory or unacceptable. Even if we don't get caught up in it directly, it can still affect us. With enough secondhand griping, we get emotional cancer. We start to perceive more injustices in our own lives. Those are Stormtroopers occupying valuable real estate in our brains and hearts.

Have you ever found that the more you complain—and the more you read and hear other people complain—the easier it is to find things to complain about? On the other hand, have you ever found that the more grateful you are, the more you have to be grateful for?

Complaining is the quintessential example of something that is "easy but trivial." In fact, it's one of the easiest things for us to do. But toxic thoughts like these, however trivial, quickly accumulate. And the more mental space they occupy, the harder it becomes to return to the Effortless State.

When you focus on something you are thankful for, the effect is instant. It immediately shifts you from a *lack state* (regrets, worries about the future, the feeling of being behind) and puts you into a *have state* (what is going right, what progress you are making, what potential exists in this moment). It reminds you of all the resources, all the assets, all the skills you have at your disposal—so you can use them to more easily do what matters most.

In the figures below and on the next page, we can see that when we focus on what we have, those things expand.

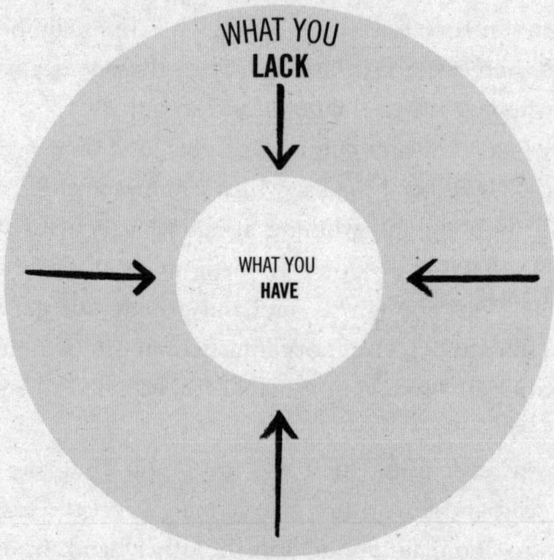

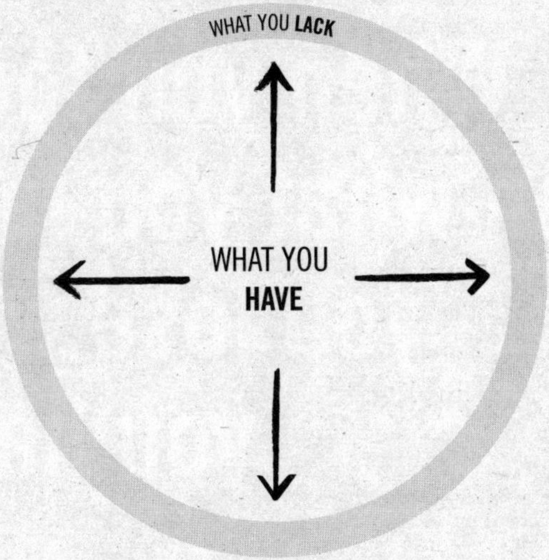

Gratitude is a powerful, catalytic thing. It starves negative emotions of the oxygen they need to survive. It also generates a positive, self-sustaining system wherever and whenever it is applied.

The *broaden-and-build theory* in psychology offers an explanation for why this is the case. Positive emotions open us to new perspectives and possibilities. Our openness encourages creative ideas and fosters social bonds. These things change us. They unlock new physical, intellectual, psychological, and social resources. They create "an upward spiral" that improves our odds of coping with the next challenge we face.

The benefits don't stop with us either: when we express gratitude to others, we see their faces light up. They seem less burdened and more expansive. A positive cycle results.

When you focus
on what you lack,
you lose what
you have.

When you focus on what you have, you get what you lack.

Complaining, too, creates a self-sustaining cycle. But instead of making it easier to do what matters, this system makes it harder. A "downward spiral." When we experience negative emotions our mindset narrows (think: fight, flight, or freeze). We are less open to new ideas and to other people. This weakens our personal physical, intellectual, and psychological resources. It depletes our reserves, making it harder to cope with the very challenges or frustrations that provoked our complaints in the first place. And so it goes.

Jim Collins uses the metaphor of a flywheel to illustrate how a self-sustaining system is created: "You're pushing no harder than during the first rotation, but the flywheel goes faster and faster." He adds, "Two turns . . . then four . . . then eight . . . the flywheel builds momentum . . . sixteen . . . thirty-two . . . moving faster . . . a thousand . . . ten thousand . . . a hundred thousand. Then at some point—breakthrough! The flywheel flies forward with almost unstoppable momentum."

Put simply, a system is self-sustaining if it requires less and less investment of energy over time. Once it's set in motion, maintaining it becomes easier, then easy, then eventually effortless.

A Recipe for Gratitude

My wife, Anna, once had a co-worker who was a real challenge. She criticized Anna continuously. She complained about their job and talked about how much she wanted to quit. It was emotionally, mentally, physically draining. But Anna was committed to her job and needed a way not just to cope but hopefully to forge a more positive, productive relationship.

It would have been easy for Anna to get pulled into the negativity. It would have been easy for her to come home in the evening and complain about the other woman's complaining. Instead, she decided to actively look for things to be grateful for in her co-worker.

At first, this was hard to do. But then Anna realized that a lot of the negatives about this woman, if looked at a little differently, could be inverted into positives.

When she talked about missing her old job, Anna could be grateful that she had positive things to say about her old job.

When she complained about something they were working on, Anna could be grateful she was *doing* the work.

When she criticized others, her observations stemmed from real intelligence. Anna could be grateful for that.

Once Anna got into the habit of looking for things to be grateful for in her co-worker, it became easier and easier to see her strengths. Then Anna was able to compliment her on those strengths. That caught her co-worker off guard. You can imagine she wasn't getting much positive feedback in general, and it seemed to improve her mood. Over time, she began to trust Anna, and they grew to become friends—not just colleagues who could tolerate each other, or even colleagues who could get things done together, but friends. And even though they no longer work together, they are friends to this day.

BJ Fogg, founder of the Behavior Design Lab at Stanford University, says that to create a new habit we simply need to look for something we already do and then attach a new behavior to it. He calls this a habit recipe, the simplest version of which is: "After [X] I will [Y]."

We can apply this idea to make gratitude a habit, by using the following recipe: *After I complain I will say something I am thankful for.*

The moment I started applying this recipe, I was shocked to realize how much I was complaining. I think of myself as a positive, optimistic person. But once I started paying attention, I realized that I was actually complaining quite a lot, often without any awareness.

So I resolved to attach gratitude to each and every complaint. When I caught myself saying, "Getting through airport security was a hassle today," I would add, "I am thankful to be safely on the plane." After grumbling, "My son didn't get to his math homework yet," I would say, "I am thankful he is so interested in the new book he is reading." After bemoaning the fact that "I was expecting to have lost more weight this week," I would add, "I am thankful I am watching my weight and my health."

After a couple of days of using this rule, I noticed I would start to catch myself midcomplaint and quickly finish my sentence with words of gratitude. It wasn't long before I would catch myself simply *thinking about* complaining—and I would think of something I was thankful for instead. At first this shift was deliberate and hard; then it was deliberate and easier; then, eventually, effortless.

Relieve a Grudge of Its Duties

Chris Williams knew what mattered in his life. His family wasn't just the most important thing; for him, it was the only thing.

Then, one freezing night in February 2007, the car he was driving was hit broadside by an erratic teenage driver. Williams's wife, their unborn baby, his nine-year-old daughter, and his eleven-year-old son were all killed. His six-year-old son was seriously injured, and his fourteen-year-old son, who was at a friend's house at the time of the crash, would never be the same after that day.

We would all expect Chris to be swallowed up, body and soul, by this experience. None of us would fault him for being overcome by fury through his grief. It's the most natural thing to imagine: his resentment closing around him, scarring him, following him around for decades. Which is what made Williams's choice in that moment so breathtaking.

Minutes after the crash, sitting amid the twisted metal and broken bodies, Williams had an eye-of-the-storm moment of clarity. Not the next day, not a year later, but right there, at this unimaginably violent scene, he saw two possible lives ahead of him.

The first future was one where he indulged his rage and bitterness, born in that moment. Choosing that future, he knew, meant he would be carrying the burden of those emotions for the rest of his life. It meant passing on those burdens to his surviving sons, inflicting emotional scars that might never heal.

The second future was one free from those burdens—one where he could be present for his surviving children as they recovered from the physical and psychological trauma they had sustained. It was one filled with purpose and meaning. It might have been the harder choice to make in that moment, but it was unquestionably the one that would lead to an easier life.

In that remarkable moment, he decided to forgive. That is not to say he did not feel anger, or did not suffer, because he did. But what he didn't do was make the suffering even harder for himself by wallowing in resentment and fury. Instead, he turned his energy, his life force, toward letting go.

Have you ever held on to a grudge against people who hurt you? Wasted precious mental energy being angry, hurt, annoyed, or resentful? How long has the wound been festering? Weeks? Months? Years? Decades?

Williams's story shows the opposite pattern. And if he could choose the path of forgiveness after the unthinkable tragedy he endured, surely we can all let go of the grudges that we have been holding on to, which have made it harder to focus on the things we truly care about.

A good first step we can take is to ask this unusual question: *What job have I hired this grudge to do?*

According to the late Clayton Christensen, a Harvard Business School professor who had been named the world's top management thinker, people don't really buy products or services. Rather, they "hire" them to do a job.

In a similar way, we often hire a grudge to fulfill an emotional need that is not currently being met. But as we conduct a performance review, we discover grudges perform poorly. Grudges cost us resources but don't deliver a satisfying return on our investment. So we must relieve a grudge of its duties.

Sometimes we hire a grudge to make us feel in control. We try to prove to ourselves and others that we are right and they are wrong. At first this can make us feel superior, even powerful. It gives us a sense of control, but one that is fleeting and false, because in reality a grudge controls you. Like Wormtongue in service to the king of Rohan in *The Lord of the Rings,* a grudge pretends to be subservient to us but really takes over. It also keeps us trapped in a never-ending loop of blame, self-righteousness, and self-loathing.

There are times we hire a grudge to give us attention. When people hear our story of victimhood, we get their support and sympathy. We are thus incentivized to tell our story again and again. This is easy and even satisfying in the moment. But it delivers an unsatisfying ending. Behind the sympathy people express, there is also fatigue. This is one reason you always have to find new people to tell your story to.

We can hire a grudge to get us off the hook. As long as we have someone to blame, we don't have to take responsibility for our anger. We are granted implicit permission to wallow in the negativity we feel, without having to justify ourselves to anyone. Again, this feels freeing in the short term, but in the long term our prize is not freedom. Our prize is living captive to our anger, resentment, contempt, and negativity.

We hire a grudge to protect ourselves. We think that by being wary of the person or people who hurt us once, we can protect ourselves from being hurt again. We think the grudge creates emotional armor. But this too turns out to be a scam. The grudge makes us more vulnerable, more fearful. It becomes harder to trust, to let anybody in.

I once worked with a highly profitable firm. They were operating at $1 million of revenue per employee. While we were discussing how to remain entrepreneurial and lean as they scaled their enterprise, I suggested a rule of thumb I thought might sound a little harsh. It was this: "Hire slow, fire fast." It is a good rule of thumb for growing a business and a good rule of thumb for building a grudge-free life. With grudges, we should hire slow (or not at all) and fire fast.

Accept What You Can't Control

The shock of the diagnosis hit my friend Jonathan Cullen like a train. His unborn son, Tristan, had Down syndrome.

After he was born, Tristan spent months in the neonatal ICU battling life-threatening health issues. Jonathan's control over the situation was waning by the day, and the more helpless he felt, the more his worry overwhelmed him.

Some of his friends stepped up: they sent meals, they called, they offered support and comfort. Yet others faded away. These reactions confused Jonathan and his wife.

Months into the ordeal, Jonathan realized he had to accept the reality of his friends' behavior. He knew he couldn't change them; all he could do was accept them for who they were.

The friends who always sprang into action and helped out in a crisis were the ones calling, sending food, anticipating what he and his wife needed without even having to ask. Meanwhile his more passive friends who tended to retreat when times got tough were the ones frozen in inaction. The behavior was probably not malicious. It certainly wasn't out of character. And maybe it shouldn't have even been that unexpected.

"When someone shows you who they are, believe them the first time," said Maya Angelou. So Jonathan decided to start believing them. He let go of his unrealistic expectations for how he wished they would behave. He accepted reality as it was and would be.

Only then could he find true acceptance: the necessary first step toward a new trajectory for his life. "For after all," as Henry Wadsworth Longfellow wrote, "the best thing one can do when it is raining, is to let it rain."

When we let go of our need to punish those who've hurt us, it's not the culprit who is freed. We are freed. When we surrender grudges and complaints in favor of grace and compassion, it's not an equal exchange. It's a coup. And with every trade, we return closer to the calm of our Effortless State.

Chapter 4

REST

The Art of Doing Nothing

Jerry Swale is an eye surgeon who tried to do it all for a long, long time. His wife recalls how he would sit with his head in his hands and say, "I can't do it all, I can't do it all!" But then he would stand up and declare, "I *have* to!" And he would desperately try to push himself to do more.

But at age fifty-six he started experiencing some health issues—like a rash on his hands that threatened to end his surgical career. He knew he needed to get to a dermatologist, but he was so busy at work, he didn't even have the space in his overscheduled life to make an appointment.

Finally, on a long road trip with his wife, he realized that space would not magically appear in his life. If he was ever going to get the medical help he needed, *he* would have to make the space for it. Which meant that for the first time in as long as he could remember, caring for himself would have to take priority over caring for his patients. So together with his wife, he worked out what he needed and how he would go about doing it.

He told everyone at the office that he needed to dial back his hours, and they were supportive.

Church was harder. But, with the new realization that he couldn't truly serve others in his fatigued state, he stepped down from the elder board and told people why. Not long after, three other overwhelmed people also stepped down. It was as though he had given them permission.

He got to a dermatologist. He started riding a bike every day, which he loved. He started getting eight hours of sleep a night—compared to the five or six hours he used to claim were "all he needed."

Soon after, his business partner retired with just a month's notice, leaving Jerry to take over all his patients. If Jerry had tried to deal with that added responsibility and workload in a burned-out state, it might well have finished him off. A year prior, "That stress might have given him a heart attack," his wife recalled.

Fortunately, with his energy restored, he was able to meet the challenge with relative ease. He was clearheaded about what he could and couldn't take on. He was able to make decisions more quickly and execute them more efficiently. Rest proved an antidote for both pre-existing and future stress. It kept him grounded in the Effortless State.

Learning to Relax

It may seem odd that we need to learn how to take a break. But in our 24/7 always-on culture, some people simply don't know how to relax. Ironically, for them, doing nothing is painfully hard. Joe Maddon, the manager of the Los Angeles Angels, has learned that professional baseball players tend to be among those people.

Maddon, who worked for the Angels for thirty-one years and who in that time held a long list of positions including manager, scout, roving hitting instructor, bench coach, and first base coach, is someone you might expect to advocate for endless hustle. Certainly, according to Maddon, a lot of players are taught to expect exactly this. He said, "Since coming up in the minors, position players are taught to arrive at the ballpark early, take batting practice on a daily basis and prepare for a game hours before the first pitch." But the baseball season is long. With 162 games, teams can go through stretches where they play almost every day for a month and a half. By the time the playoffs come in the fall, many players are spent.

However, Maddon sees the advantage of a different approach. He said, "I didn't have enough chance to do nothing last offseason. I want more of an opportunity to do nothing, and I mean that in a positive way. When you get this downtime, to be able to do nothing well, that's my goal."

One way he has implemented the art of doing nothing with his players is by instigating "American Legion Week." The week is held during the dog days of August, when player performance often dips. But instead of cramming in hours of pregame practice, he told his players to just show up for the game. He encouraged them to sleep in, take naps, and arrive fresh, the same way they did when they were teenagers, as amateurs.

It's not that Maddon isn't interested in his players performing at their best. Of course, he wants a team of elite players playing the best baseball of their careers. He simply believes that regular spurts of "doing nothing" are the best way to achieve that. He said, "If you treat it that way, it keeps their minds fresher. And if their mind is fresher, they'll play a better game."

Maddon's approach has had a transformative impact not only on the Angels but on the other teams he's coached over the past decade as well. After he launched American Legion Week with Tampa

Bay, the Devil Rays made it to the World Series within a year. When he brought it with him to Chicago, the Cubs won the most games in the league over the next four years, including the World Series in 2016. Incredibly, over a five-year period, Maddon's Cubs won twenty-one of twenty-four games during American Legion Week.

Recent research in physiology supports Maddon's counterintuitive response. Studies show that peak physical and mental performance requires a rhythm of exerting and renewing energy—and not just for athletes. In fact, one study found that the best-performing athletes, musicians, chess players, and writers all honed their skills in the same way: by practicing in the morning, in three sessions of sixty to ninety minutes, with breaks in between. Meanwhile, those who took fewer or shorter breaks performed less well.

Relaxing is a responsibility.

"To maximize gains from long-term practice," the study's lead author, K. Anders Ericsson, concluded, "individuals must avoid exhaustion and must limit practice to an amount from which they can completely recover on a daily or weekly basis."

Many of us struggle with the tension between not doing enough and doing too much. Have you ever pushed yourself so far past the point of exhaustion one day that you wake up the next morning utterly depleted and need the entire day to rest? To stop this vicious cycle in its tracks, try this simple rule: Do not do more today than you can completely recover from today. Do not do more this week than you can completely recover from this week.

We can miss the signs that we've reached the end of an energy cycle. We can ignore the loss of focus, low energy, and fidgeting. We can power through. We can artificially try to compensate with caffeine or sugar to get past our energy slump. But in the end, our fatigue catches up with us, making essential work much harder than it needs to be.

The easier way is to replenish our physical and mental energy continuously by taking short breaks. We can plan those breaks into our day. We can be like the peak performers who take advantage of their bodies' natural rhythm.

We can do the following:

1. Dedicate mornings to essential work.
2. Break down that work into three sessions of no more than ninety minutes each.
3. Take a short break (ten to fifteen minutes) in between sessions to rest and recover.

The Power of the One-Minute Pause

Katrín Davíðsdóttir is a native of Reykjavík, Iceland. A gymnast turned CrossFit competitor, her goal was to be the fittest woman in the world by winning the CrossFit World Championship.

In 2014, when she was just inches away from reaching the world championship, she stalled. Every muscle in her arms was straining. One more pull skyward and she'd be there. But she lost her grip. She came crashing down to the floor.

She was allowed to try again. But by this point she had broken down, emotionally and mentally. She tried again but couldn't do it. So she gave up.

The following year, Davíðsdóttir decided to hire Ben Bergeron as her coach.

When I spoke with Bergeron on my podcast, I asked him about that 2014 competition. He told me that if at that stalled moment she had taken even one minute to rest physically and reset mentally before resuming, she would have finished the climb and made it into the finals. Think about that: taking just one minute to get into the right state, the Effortless State, in order to take advantage of the body's amazing ability to rapidly recover would have made all the difference for her on that day.

So Bergeron immediately shifted her approach. Her entire life became about five things: training, recovery, nutrition, sleep, and mindset. And the results have been remarkable.

That year, with Bergeron as her coach, Davíðsdóttir not only qualified for the championship games but became the 2015 champion. She was crowned Fittest Woman on Earth. The following year, 2016, she did it again. In fact, as of this writing she has finished in the Top 5 every year for the past five years.

When we are struggling, instead of doubling down on our efforts, we might consider pausing the action—even for one minute. We don't need to fight these natural rhythms. We can flow with them. We can use them to our advantage. We can alternate between periods of exertion and renewal.

Lack of Sleep Is Killing Us

Does it sometimes seem like you're sleeping a lot less than you used to? Collectively we all are; research shows that today we get less sleep—almost two hours less on average—than fifty years ago. This is not inconsequential. People who sleep less than seven hours a night are more likely to suffer from cardiovascular disease, heart attack, stroke, asthma, arthritis, depression, and diabetes and are almost eight times more likely to be overweight.

Sleep deprivation is insidious. In one study, people who got less than six hours of sleep per night saw a decline in their motor skills and their cognitive abilities and nodded off more frequently. No surprise. But even more concerning was the finding that we are quite bad at noticing the cumulative impact sleep deprivation has on our minds and bodies.

We tend to think that after a few nights in a row of insufficient sleep we can simply reset; we tell ourselves all we need is one solid night to "catch up." But as this study revealed, we are actually racking up "sleep debt" for every night we don't get the ideal seven or eight hours of shut-eye. By day 10, subjects had racked up so much sleep debt, they were experiencing the same effects as the participants who had not slept for an entire night. While they claimed to feel "only slightly sleepy," their performance suggested otherwise. As the study's author explains, "Routine nightly sleep for fewer than six hours results in cognitive performance deficits, even if we feel we have adapted to it."

Getting more sleep may be the single greatest gift we can give our bodies, our minds, and even, it turns out, our bottom lines.

Go Deep

Sean Wise is a professor of entrepreneurship at Ryerson University in Toronto, Canada. Over his two decades in the venture capital industry, where he specialized in supporting high-growth ventures at the seed stage, he has worked with many highly driven founders operating in high-risk, high-pressure environments. In other words, he knows a lot of people who don't get enough sleep.

The Silicon Valley mythology would have us believe that the

founders of the most disruptive, world-changing companies have no time for something as trivial as sleep. After all, the origin stories of most successful start-ups tend to involve caffeine-fueled founders coding in a trance-like state for days and nights on end, until they ultimately emerge, pale and wild-eyed from lack of sleep, with their billion-dollar idea. Wise's observations differ substantially from this narrative. "I have seen firsthand that poor sleep quality and/or an insufficient sleep quantity undermines the mindsets of founders," he says, "making them harder to work with and less resilient, which in turn reduces the probability of startup success." This is not surprising when you consider the research showing that sleep problems may undermine alertness, creativity, and social competence—all critical qualities for high-striving entrepreneurs.

Having seen firsthand how better sleep quality leads to more innovative thinking, Wise decided to experiment with his own sleep. He wanted to see if he could improve not just the amount of sleep he was getting but also its quality. Specifically, he wanted to increase both his ratio of "deep sleep" to lighter sleep and his amount of uninterrupted sleep.

Research shows that Wise's goals were well chosen. Deep sleep is crucial to many aspects of health; even if we manage a full night's sleep, unless enough of that sleep is in a deep state, we'll suffer from sleep deprivation. Unlike in rapid eye movement (REM) sleep, in the deep sleep stage, your body and brain waves slow down. This is the stage where information is stored in long-term memory, learning and emotions are processed, the immune system is energized, and the body recovers. Healthy adults spend an average of 13 to 23 percent of their night in deep sleep. So if you sleep for seven hours, that translates to just fifty to one hundred minutes in a deep state. Each minute, in other words, is precious.

Sleep quality, on the other hand, is how much uninterrupted sleep you get overall. Uninterrupted sleep is when our brain waves and heart rate reach a point that allows physiological and psychological resources to be restored. This is why we rarely feel rested when we wake up a number of times at night.

To try to maximize both deep sleep and sleep quality, Wise took some simple steps. He went to bed at the same time every night, turned off digital devices an hour before bed, and before turning in, took a hot shower. He then tracked his sleep on his smartwatch for a month. He noted his heart rate, time in bed, time asleep, quality of sleep, and percentage of deep sleep.

Why the hot shower? Recent sleep science found that participants who used water-based passive body heating—also known as a bath—before bed slept sooner, longer, and better. This seems counterintuitive considering that our sleep cycles are associated with a drop in core body temperature. But according to this research, the key is the timing of the bath or shower: ninety minutes before bedtime. The lead author explains that the warm water triggers our body's cooling mechanism, sending warmer blood from our core outward and shedding heat through our hands and feet. This "efficient removal of body heat and decline in body temperature" speeds up the natural cooling that makes it easier to fall asleep.

After four weeks Wise's deep sleep shot up to almost two hours a night, an 800 percent increase. His uninterrupted sleep went up 20 percent. He felt sharper, more creative, and more present. He woke up feeling refreshed and ready to tackle another day.

As Wise points out, "We spend a third of our lives asleep. Perhaps it is time for you to evaluate if you could be doing it better."

Take an Effortless Nap

I'll admit I don't always get the optimal amount of deep or quality sleep at night. But I am a champion napper. Luckily for me, research shows that naps can counter this sleep debt. In fact, naps can improve performance in reaction time, logical reasoning, and symbol recognition even in well-rested people. They can improve mood, making us less impulsive and frustrated. In one study, a nap was as beneficial for some types of memory as a full night's sleep. "What's amazing is that in a 90-minute nap, you can get the same [learning] benefits as an eight-hour sleep period," the researcher says.

The idea of taking regular naps is appealing to most people I have spoken with. Yet they find it almost impossible to do in practice. What makes it so hard?

We are conditioned to feel guilty when we nap instead of "getting things done." It's a perfect storm of the fear of missing out, the false economy of powering through, and the stigma of napping as something just plain lazy or even childish.

Much has been written about the corrosive effects of today's hustle culture in which we wear comments like "I just don't need a lot of sleep" or "Who has the time to sleep?! Not me!" as a badge of honor. But in fact, "sleep shaming" is a timeless tradition. The historian and presidential biographer Ron Chernow tells the story of how, when US Civil War hero Ulysses S. Grant attempted to go to bed at 11:00 P.M. the night before an important battle, one of his commanders pointedly reminded him that Napoleon indulged in only four hours of sleep every night and still preserved all the vigor of his mental faculties. Grant, who regularly got seven hours, was dubious and replied, "Well I for one never believed those stories. If truth were known, I have no doubt that it would be found that he made up for his short sleep at night by taking naps during the day."

It's about time we started thinking about naps differently. The recipe for taking an Effortless Nap is as follows:

1. Notice when your fatigue has gotten to the point that you feel it is real work to concentrate.

2. Block out light and noise using an eye mask and a noise canceller or earplugs.
3. Set an alarm for a desired time.
4. As you try to fall asleep, banish all thoughts about what you "could be doing." Your to-do's will all still be there when you wake up. Only now, you'll be able to get them done faster, and with greater ease.

The first few times, this may take some effort. You may not actually fall asleep. But keep trying. Once you've figured out the time of day you're likely to need a nap, block your calendar for it. With some practice, naps will become effortless—and guilt-free.

Slumber with a Key

Salvador Dalí's best-known painting, *The Persistence of Memory,* appears to be set in a realistic rocky landscape of Dalí's native Catalonia. But like much of surrealist art, the piece has a bizarre dreamlike quality. Clocks have lost their integrity and melt in the sun like Camembert cheese. A lone fly produces a shadow with a human form. A swarm of ants gather. Painted at the height of the surrealist movement in 1931, the work catapulted Dalí into global prominence.

Dalí's influences were the art of the impressionist period and the Renaissance. His formal education was in fine arts in Madrid. Given this background, we would expect Dalí to have painted accurate, lifelike depictions. How, then, did he break free from these classical techniques to create haunting juxtapositions between reality and dreams?

He napped—at least the surrealist version of a nap. Dalí would sit in a chair, wrists dangling over the edges of the armrests. In one hand, he would grip a heavy metal key between his thumb and forefinger. On the floor, directly underneath the key, he would place an upside-down plate. Dalí would close his eyes and relax. The moment he drifted off to sleep, his grip on the key would release. Clang! Dalí's eyes would snap open. And he would be filled with new inspiration for his next strange work. Dalí explained that in that "fugitive moment when you had barely lost consciousness and during which you cannot be assured of having really slept" he was "in equilibrium on the taut and invisible wire that separates sleep from waking." Dalí called his technique "slumber with a key."

Dreams are fertile ground for creative solutions to what burdens us all day. But we often wake up with only wisps of ideas that quickly vanish if we fail to capture them. If you are seeking inspiration, the easiest thing you can do is rest your eyes. Sit in your favorite chair. Whether you use an alarm or a key, keep a pencil handy and write down whatever comes to mind when your eyes snap open.

When we end our war on our body's natural rhythms, when we let others pass us in the unwinnable race for the most achieved with the least rest, our lives gain texture, clarity, and intention. We return to our Effortless State.

Chapter 5

NOTICE

How to See Clearly

Sir Arthur Conan Doyle's character Sherlock Holmes is among the best-known and most widely portrayed literary characters in film and television history. So it might surprise you to learn that the private detective appeared in only four of Doyle's forty-five novels. Part of what makes his character so compelling and so memorable is his unparalleled skill of observation. His keenest ability is to notice the tiniest of details the rest of us miss. It's an ability illustrated and discussed in Doyle's 1891 short story "A Scandal in Bohemia."

The story begins with perennial narrator Dr. John H. Watson visiting his friend Holmes at his famous 221B Baker Street, London, address. Holmes surprises Watson, asking, "How do I know that you have been getting yourself very wet lately, and that you have a most clumsy and careless servant girl?" Dumbfounded, Watson confirms that he took a country walk earlier in the week and indeed returned muddy. But he cannot understand how Holmes could possibly have known such a thing. Holmes responds that it is "simplicity itself": on the inside of Watson's left shoe, just where the light from a fire would land, the leather is scored by six almost parallel cuts. Holmes reasons that the marks were caused by a careless assistant scraping mud from the shoe by firelight.

Watson asks Holmes why his explanations seem so obvious, yet so out of reach until shared. "I believe that my eyes are as good as yours," Watson says. "Quite so," Holmes responds, throwing himself down into an armchair. "You see, but you do not observe." Holmes then asks him how many steps there are leading up from the hall downstairs. Watson has traversed this staircase hundreds of times. Yet he has no answer. "You have not observed," Holmes says, triumphant. "And yet you have seen."

As Watson reflects on this conversation, he says, "The exchange really shook me. Feverishly, I tried to remember how many steps there were in our own house, how many led up to our front door (I couldn't). And for a long time afterward, I tried to count stairs and steps whenever I could, lodging the proper number in my memory in case anyone ever called upon me to report. I'd make Holmes proud (of course, I'd promptly forget each number I had so diligently tried to remember—and it wasn't until later that I realized that by focusing so intently on memorization, I'd missed the point entirely and was actually being less, not more observant)."

Many of us can easily relate to the distress Watson articulates in this story. After all, who among us hasn't had the experience of someone pointing out something painfully obvious, ever-present, or easily observable in our environment that we have never noticed? Watson viewed Holmes's seemingly superhuman ability to deduce a series of accurate facts from seemingly insignificant clues as something akin to magic. But of course, this is not magic. It is the difference between seeing and observing, between watching and noticing, between being and being present.

How often do we engage in the act of observing, of truly *noticing*? I know many people who struggle with this. It feels hard to be present in the moment, to be laser focused on one person or conversation or experience, when we are constantly juggling so many other demands on our attention. But what makes it seem difficult is not the task itself.

Listening isn't hard; it's stopping our mind from wandering that's hard.

Being in the moment isn't hard; not thinking about the past and future all the time is hard.

It's not the noticing itself that's hard. It's ignoring all the noise in our environment that is hard.

At least it is at first. But once we remove some of the thoughts, the worries, and the external distractions clouding our vision, we see that Holmes's "magic" becomes a little easier.

These distractions are like cataracts in your eyes. Left untreated, cataracts only multiply and worsen; and with them, so does your vision. It becomes harder to read. You have to strain to see the person you're speaking with. It's not safe to get behind the wheel. The less light that gets into the retina, the harder everything becomes. Ultimately, cataracts can lead to total blindness.

Distractions that keep us from being present in the moment can be like cataracts for our minds. They make noticing what matters harder. And the longer they are left untreated, the more debilitating they become. Less and less light comes in. We miss more and more. Eventually we become blind to what really matters most.

Fortunately, cataracts can be removed. As we remove the cataract, the light gets to the retina again, and we can see the things we were missing before, clearly and easily.

How to See Clearly

Steph Curry had always dreamed of playing basketball for his father's alma mater, Virginia Tech. But the college wasn't willing to offer him a scholarship, partly because of his size. At "only" six foot three and 185 pounds, Curry was at an immediate disadvantage in a sport where players had been getting bigger and bigger. In 2009, the year Curry was drafted by the Golden State Warriors, the average height for an NBA player was just under six foot seven. Los Angeles Lakers superstar LeBron James was a towering six foot nine, and weighing in at over 300 pounds, Shaquille O'Neal tore down entire backboards.

Small NBA players typically train their agility and quickness. But Curry took a different approach; he opted to focus on training his brain.

Since his second season in 2010, trainer Brandon Payne has been putting Curry through "neurological drills" to improve his perceptive abilities. Here's an example of a drill sequence that gets progressively harder: Curry juggles a tennis ball with one hand while dribbling a basketball with the other; then he switches to dribbling the tennis ball; then he tosses the tennis ball against the wall while continuing to dribble the basketball; then he crosses the basketball between his legs; and so on until, finally, he's juggling two tennis balls. This dizzying exercise is designed to improve Curry's attention by building what Payne calls "neurocognitive efficiency." With each drill in the sequence, he's processing more and more information while remaining focused on the task.

In an article titled "Steph Curry Literally Sees the World Differently Than You Do," reporter Drake Baer writes, "Just by looking at Curry, you would never guess that he's the most dominant player in the league. He's six-foot-three, 190 lbs. He doesn't bulldoze like LeBron or fly like Michael. His advantages are subtler. The remarkable quickness and off-the-charts shooting skills are ones that everyone knows about already. But the evidence also points to Curry being an extreme outlier—it wouldn't be wrong to say genius—in his ability to process sensory input, even in the most stressful, complex, and fast-moving situations. In simplistic terms, he's seeing more of the game, allowing him to exploit opponents' positioning to create shots, find passing lanes, and force turnovers." Warriors coach Steve Kerr says that with regard to hand-eye coordination Curry is "as great as anyone I've ever seen." And Curry is now widely regarded as the best shooter in NBA history.

Recent science helps explain why. One study found that by training our attentional muscles we can improve our processing of complex information moving at great speed. Professional athletes from the English Premier League, the National Hockey League, and the French Rugby League as well as elite nonprofessional athletes and nonathletes participated in a virtual simulation with eight balls that crisscrossed and bounced off each other and the virtual walls. They were told to follow the trajectory of four of them, and when the balls stopped, the participants had to identify the ones they had followed. If they did so correctly, the simulation sped up in the next round, exactly as in Payne's drills with Curry. The results revealed, perhaps unsurprisingly, that professional athletes were better at processing complex, fast-moving information than the other groups. But even more useful for those of us unlikely to make the NBA was the fact that *all* groups improved, very quickly, with practice. *Everyone* got better at focusing on the important and ignoring the irrelevant.

To be in the Effortless State is to be aware, alert, and present, even in the face of fast-moving information and the endless onslaught of distractions. And that's no small thing, because in that state of heightened attention we see differently. We are able to laser in on the things that are important. We notice things that were always right under our noses but that we missed before.

The Inner Game of Relationship Tennis

Too often we are with people physically but are still not present with them mentally. We struggle to truly notice them, to see them clearly.

John Gottman has spent forty years researching the science of relationships at what is officially called the Gottman Institute and is otherwise known as the Love Lab. He and his wife, Julie Schwartz Gottman, a respected psychologist in her own right, have written several books and are world-renowned experts on the topics of marriage and relationships. Together they may have gathered more data on the intricate workings of relationships and on the dynamics that predict divorce versus marital stability than anyone else in the field.

According to the Gottmans, we all make small and large attempts to obtain affection, affirmation, and attention in our relationships. They call these bids for connection. There are three distinct ways a partner can respond to a bid for attention. We can liken these three approaches to playing a game of tennis.

The first type of response is what they call "turning toward." It's when you come home, give your beloved a peck on the cheek, and say something like "It's lovely weather today, isn't it." And your beloved might reply, "Oh, I agree. Isn't it beautiful! Perhaps we should open some windows." Here your partner is like the person on the other side of the court receiving your serve and hitting a solid ground stroke straight to where you are standing. It couldn't be easier to hit the ball back, and so the volley continues.

The second kind of response is "turning against." This is where your partner might respond to your comment about the weather by saying, "You really think so? I think it's much too hot out today. I don't enjoy this humidity at all!" In this case, they have hit the ball back over the net, but to the complete opposite side of the court, where you have to sprint to reach it. The volley might continue, but it's more strenuous.

The third kind of response is "turning away." Now your partner doesn't address the comment about the weather at all and instead responds with something entirely unrelated, like "Have you taken the car for the oil change yet?" The ball has just been hit straight into the net. Game over. Now you have to harness the energy (mental and physical) to start the volley anew.

According to Gottman's research, both of the first two responses—even the argumentative one—are generally healthy for a relationship. The one that does the most damage is the third kind. It signals that these two people do not see each other. They are not playing the same game, or even the same sport. It's as though they are both looking at the same wall, and one says, "This wall is blue" while the other insists that it's red.

There is no such thing as an effortless relationship. But there are ways we can make it easier to keep a relationship strong. We don't need to agree with the other person on everything. But we do need to be present with them, to really notice them, to give them our full attention—maybe not always, but as frequently as we can. Being present is, as Eckhart Tolle has said, "ease itself."

The Curious Power of Presence

Ronald Epstein felt his anxiety spike as an older doctor walked in and examined his ears, throat, neck, chest, and abdomen in what was an unremarkable visit in every way but one. The diagnosis, prognosis, and prescribed course of treatment were unsurprising and were delivered in less time than it had taken Epstein to eat breakfast that morning. But here's the remarkable thing: the doctor had sat in that examination room and answered the nervous seventeen-year-old's questions as if there were no other patients on his schedule that day.

As Epstein went to sleep that night he was already changed by the experience—although he didn't fully understand how.

The experience stayed with him during his two-week recovery from what turned out to be nothing more than a typical cold and virus. It stayed with him as he met with guidance counselors and answered the banal questions all adults ask all teenagers about what they plan to do after high school, and as he filled out the essays on college applications. And it was still with him as he trudged around campus heaving a backpack heavy enough to weigh down his body but not his spirit. He was far too focused on what he felt certain had become his calling: to learn all that he could about helping sick people heal.

Incredibly, his brief encounter with one physician years earlier—the doctor's palpable kindness, his reassuring calm, his full and utter presence—had stayed with Epstein through all of those years and was with him still.

Can a fleeting moment leave such a lasting trace as to shape the trajectory of a life? Was Epstein's whole future determined by this one doctor who sat there and listened, giving Epstein the full power of his attention?

When we're fully present with people, it has an impact. Not just in that moment either. The experience of feeling like the most important person in the world even for the briefest of moments can stay with us for a disproportionate time after the moment has passed. There is a curiously magical power of presence.

In packed conference halls and ballrooms, I have on many occasions asked audiences to think of someone who was completely present with them in their life, then describe what that was like for them in one word. I have learned not to be surprised by the volume, strength, and variety of the adjectives offered.

Words include *generous, valued, understanding, refreshing, authentic, worthy, peaceful, important, special, splendid, seen, symbiotic, focused, raw, intimate, important, invigorating, empowering, quiet, golden, magical, warm, impactful, engaging, validating, accepting,* and *priceless.*

What are we to make of these one-word stories? These are not timid descriptions. You would think these people were describing someone who had moved mountains for them. But they weren't. They were describing a person who was fully present for them.

When we are fully present with another person, we see them more clearly. And we help them see themselves more clearly as well.

The Clearness Committee

We all have people in our lives who come to us because they are struggling to see a problem or decision clearly. But often we unwittingly make it harder for them by jumping to judgment. We are too eager to say, "Oh, you should X," or "I don't know why you didn't do Y in the first place," or "If I were you I would Z." Such quick judgments, however well intentioned, make it harder for people to gain clarity, for two reasons.

First, when people fear being judged, it drowns out their inner voice. They are able to focus only on what they think we want to hear, rather than on what they actually see or feel. Second, the moment our judgments and opinions are voiced, they compete for the limited mental space others need to draw their own conclusions.

Contrast this with a practice used by the Quakers called the Clearness Committee.

When someone in the community (the "focus person") is facing an important dilemma, they often ask a few people they trust (the "Elders") to come together to form a committee. The purpose is not for the committee to tell them what to do. The purpose is to help them figure it out for themselves. And in order to do this, the committee must remove judgment from the equation.

When they gather, the focus person begins by sharing what the dilemma is and why it matters. The committee listens silently.

After the context is given, the Elders have a few choices: they can ask "honest questions," which are clarifying questions they could not know the answer to. They can reflect or repeat back what they have heard. Opinions, advice, and judgment are out-of-bounds.

As Parker Palmer, an expert in the Clearness Committee process, has written, "Each of us has an inner teacher, a voice of truth, that offers the guidance and power we need to deal with our problems." The intent of the exercise is to help people amplify this inner voice and gain clarity on how to move forward.

We can help people in our lives do the same by putting aside our own opinions, advice, or judgment completely, by putting the other person's truth above our own.

The greatest gift we can offer to others is not our skill or our money or our effort. It is simply *us.* None of us have infinite reserves of focus and attention to give away. But in the Effortless State, it becomes far easier to give the gift of our intentional focus to the people and things we really care about.

How can we call up this state of heightened perception and focus on demand? I recommend the following daily practice.

1: Prepare Your Space (two minutes)

Find a quiet place. Turn off your phone. Let people know you will be taking ten minutes.

Take a moment to clear off your desk. To put things back in their proper place.

2: Rest Your Body (two minutes)

Sit comfortably with your back straight. Close your eyes. Roll your shoulders. Move your head from side to side. Release tension in every part of your body. Breathe normally and naturally.

3: Relax Your Mind (two minutes)

It's natural for your mind to be full of thoughts. Just acknowledge them. Notice them. Let them come and let them go.

4: Release Your Heart (two minutes)

If thoughts of someone who has wronged you arise, say, "I forgive you," and imagine you are cutting a chain that tethers you to them.

5: Breathe in Gratitude (two minutes)

Relive a moment in your life that you are really thankful for. Experience it again, using all of your senses. Remember where you were, how you felt, and who you were with. Really breathe the gratitude in. Repeat this step three times.

An Effortless Summary

Part I	Effortless State
What is the Effortless State?	The Effortless State is an experience many of us have had when we are physically rested, emotionally unburdened, and mentally energized. You are completely aware, alert, present, attentive, and focused on what's important in this moment. You are able to focus on what matters most with ease.
INVERT	Instead of asking, "Why is this so hard?," invert the question by asking, "What if this could be easy?" Challenge the assumption that the "right" way is, inevitably, the harder one. Make the impossible possible by finding an indirect approach. When faced with work that feels overwhelming, ask, "How am I making this harder than it needs to be?"
ENJOY	Pair the most essential activities with the most enjoyable ones. Accept that work and play can co-exist. Turn tedious tasks into meaningful rituals. Allow laughter and fun to lighten more of your moments.
RELEASE	Let go of emotional burdens you don't need to keep carrying. Remember: When you focus on what you lack, you lose what you have. When you focus on what you have, you get what you lack. Use this habit recipe: "Each time I complain I will say something I am thankful for." Relieve a grudge of its duties by asking, "What job have I hired this grudge to do?"
REST	Discover the art of doing nothing. Do not do more today than you can completely recover from by tomorrow. Break down essential work into three sessions of no more than ninety minutes each. Take an effortless nap.

NOTICE	Achieve a state of heightened awareness by harnessing the power of presence. Train your brain to focus on the important and ignore the irrelevant. To see others more clearly, set aside your opinions, advice, and judgment, and put their truth above your own. Clear the clutter in your physical environment before clearing the clutter in your mind.

effortless action

PART II

Larry Silverberg is a "dynamicist" at North Carolina State University. That simply means he is an expert in the movement of physical things. For example, he has studied the movement of millions of free throws over twenty years.

One thing he has found over the years is that the most important factor for successfully shooting a free throw is the speed at which you release the ball. To achieve the kinesthetic sweet spot takes practice and muscle memory. The goal is to get to the point where you try without trying—where your movement becomes smooth, natural, and instinctive.

That is what is meant by *Effortless Action*.

If you try too hard when shooting a free throw, you'll tense up and move too fast. This is similar to what happens to many overachievers who have been conditioned to believe that more effort leads to better outcomes. When they invest a lot of effort and don't see the results they want, they lean in harder. They work longer hours. They obsess over the situation more. They are trained to see the lack of progress as a sign that yet *more* effort is required. What they haven't learned is that:

Past a certain point, more effort doesn't produce better performance. It sabotages our performance.

Economists call this the law of ***diminishing returns:*** after a certain point, each extra unit of input produces a decreasing rate of output. For example, if I write for two hours I can produce two pages. But if I write for four hours I can produce three pages. The rate of output is slowing down. More effort at this point should be questioned. But sometimes overachievers double down on effort. They see the reduced output and mistakenly think the answer is to push even harder. What is the effect of this?

Past a certain point, more effort doesn't produce better performance. It sabotages our performance.

Negative returns: the point where we are not merely getting a smaller return on each additional investment, we are actually *decreasing* our overall output. For example, there is a point in writing where you start making a manuscript worse by working on it

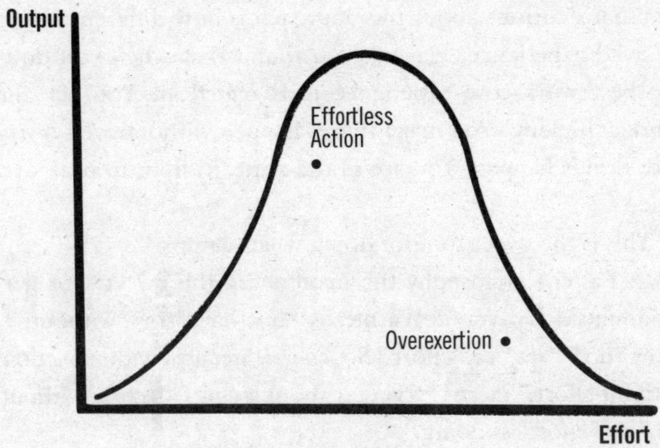

longer. The same can be said for composing a song, drafting a blueprint, preparing a legal argument, or writing computer code, along with many other endeavors. You are fatigued. Your judgment is impaired. Every ounce of extra effort you put in now is detrimental. It is an example of *false economy* to continue at this point.

It's not just that overall output suffers; it's a recipe for burnout as well.

This is an example of overexertion, or in everyday parlance, trying too hard. Perhaps you have experienced this yourself. Trying too hard in a social setting makes it harder to connect authentically with someone else. Trying too hard for a promotion can reek of desperation and, therefore, make you seem less desirable. Trying too hard to get to sleep can make it almost impossible to wind down. Trying too hard to look intelligent rarely impresses the people you want to impress. Trying too hard to be cool, to relax, to feel good, all make it harder to be cool, relax, or feel good. That's the trouble with overexertion.

What's curious about this approach is how different it is from our lived experience. Haven't you found that when you do your very best work, the experience feels effortless? You act almost without thinking. You make things happen without even *trying* to make things happen. You are in the zone, in flow, in peak performance.

This is the sweet spot for doing what matters.

In Eastern philosophy the masters call this sweet spot *wu wei* (pronounced Oo-Way). *Wu* means "not have" or "without." *Wei* means "do," "act," or "effort." So *wu wei,* literally "without action" or "without effort," means "trying without trying," "action without action," or "effortless doing."

The goal is to accomplish what matters by trying less, not more: to achieve our purpose with bridled intention, not overexertion. This is what is meant by Effortless Action.

CHAPTER 6

DEFINE

What "Done" Looks Like

Four hundred years ago, Gustav II, the king of Sweden, saw the vital need to upgrade his armada of ships. He wanted to protect his people from the growing naval powers that surrounded them. His attention was drawn to building a giant military warship. He found a shipbuilder, Henrik Hybertsson, and tasked him to build what became known as the *Vasa*.

This project was of utmost importance to King Gustav—so much so that he allocated a forest of one thousand trees to provide the lumber for the project. He opened the royal coffers too. He assured Hybertsson that he would have an almost unlimited budget to complete the project successfully.

Unfortunately, the king did not have a clear vision of what the final product would look like. Or rather, he kept changing his vision of what the final product would look like. At first the ship was to be 108 feet long with thirty-two cannons on deck. Later the length was changed to 120 feet, even though the lumber had already been cut to the original specifications. But no sooner had Henrik's team made the necessary adjustments than the target shifted again. This time, the king decided that the ship needed to be 135 feet long. The cannon requirements changed as well. Instead of thirty-two cannons in a single row, he asked for "36 cannons in 2 rows, plus another 12 small cannons, 48 mortars, and 10 other smaller caliber weapons."

Tremendous effort was exerted by some four hundred people to make this happen. But even as they approached completion, the king changed his mind again, asking for sixty-four large cannons instead. The stress of the news is said to have given Henrik a fatal heart attack.

Still, the endless project continued, this time under Henrik's assistant, Hein Jacobsson. Budgets continued to escalate. The effort continued to expand. And the king continued changing the end goal. In an utterly nonessential addition for a gunship, he even asked for some seven hundred ornate sculptures—which would take a team of expert sculptors more than two years to complete—to be attached to the sides, the bulwark, and the transom of the ship.

And so it was that on August 10, 1628, the *Vasa* left the Stockholm port for its maiden voyage still unfinished and before it had been properly tested to ensure it could survive the conditions of the high seas. Meanwhile, the king *had* found the time to plan a celebration to commemorate the expedition; there were fireworks, there were foreign diplomats, there was pageantry: "As the ship sailed away, the gun-ports were open and the guns were pointing out so that they could fire a salute to the dignitaries on shore."

Then suddenly, a gust of wind caught the sails of the ship, causing the massive vessel to tilt severely over to one side. As the cannons tipped into the sea, water entered through the gunports. Despite a strenuous, all-out effort on the part of the crew, water almost instantly flooded onto the gun deck and into the hold, further destabilizing the ship. Tragically, it took just fifty minutes for the *Vasa* to completely sink, taking fifty-three crew members with it. They died less than three-quarters of a mile from the shore.

And so the most expensive naval project in Sweden's history sailed less than a mile before being buried in the sea—all because the king had made the project almost impossible to safely complete by constantly redefining what "done" looked like.

If you want to make something hard, indeed truly impossible, to complete, all you have to do is make the end goal as vague as possible. That's because you cannot, by definition, complete a project without a clearly defined end point. You can spin your wheels working on it. You can tinker with it. You can (and likely will) abandon it. But to get an important project *done* it's absolutely necessary to define what "done" looks like.

This insight may sound obvious. But if you think of most of the essential projects you are working on, how clear is your idea of what completion looks like?

The Heavy Cost of Light Tinkering

Sometimes important projects remain undone because we keep tinkering with them endlessly. For example, my editor once received a compelling book proposal from an agent. She read it. The next day she received a new version, with an email saying, "The authors made some changes." She read the new version, which seemed more or less identical. Two days later she got *another* version, which was somehow less polished than the first. The author couldn't stop tinkering.

Whether we're writing a book proposal, putting together a presentation for clients, building a ship, or doing anything else, tinkering can improve things significantly—at first. But there comes a point where the law of diminishing returns sets in—a point where our efforts begin to outpace our improvements. I define "done" as the point just before the effort invested begins to be greater than the output achieved.

To avoid diminishing returns on your time and effort, establish clear conditions for what "done" looks like, get there, then stop.

One Minute to Clarity

We all have essential projects we want to complete. But often we find ourselves spinning our wheels, unable to get our project over the line. Often, the solution is simply to decide what "getting it over the line" actually looks like.

Getting clear on what "done" looks like doesn't just help you finish; it also helps you get started. All too often, we procrastinate or struggle to take the first steps on a project because we don't have a clear finish line in mind. As soon as you define what "done" looks like, you give your conscious and unconscious mind a clear instruction. Things click into gear and you can begin charting a course toward that end state.

It's surprising how much clarity on this you can achieve in a one-minute burst of concentration. For example, when you have an important project to deliver, take sixty seconds to close your eyes and actually visualize what it would look like to cross it off as done: "I've addressed each of the questions the client posed and proofread it once." It takes only one minute of concentration to clarify what "done" looks like.

Getting the outcome clear focuses you like nothing else can. All of your resources shift into gear to bring that outcome to fruition.

Vague Goals	What "Done" Looks Like
"Lose weight."	I look down at the weighing scale and see the number 177 staring back at me.
"Walk more."	Reach ten thousand steps a day on my Fitbit for fourteen days in a row.
"Read more books."	On my digital book reader it will say, "Finished," next to *War and Peace.*
"Turn in the big report."	Type up twelve pages full of concrete examples and actionable advice and be able to picture the customer saying, "It's terrific!"
"Launch my product."	Have ten beta users try the app for a week and give feedback.
"Complete podcast episode."	The podcast is recorded and the file is uploaded.

Make a "Done for the Day" List

"Done" isn't always going to apply to an individual task or project. We have all experienced the overwhelmed feeling that comes from staring down the barrel of a seemingly infinite "to do" list—one that has usually become longer by the end of the day than it was at the beginning. It creates an unwinnable war. So how do we know when the work of the day is "done"? Anna and I like to use a "Done for the Day" list.

A Done for the Day list is not a list of everything we theoretically *could* do today, or a list of everything we would *love* to get done. These things will inevitably extend far beyond the limited time available. Instead, this is a list of what will constitute meaningful and essential progress. As you write the list, one test is to imagine how you will feel once this work is completed. Ask yourself, "If

I complete everything on this list, will it leave me feeling satisfied by the end of the day? Is there some other important task that will haunt me all night if I don't get to it?" If your answer to the second question is yes, that is a task that should go on the Done for the Day list.

The Gift of Nothing Left Undone

"Swedish Death Cleaning" means getting rid of the clutter you have accumulated through your life while you are still alive. It's an alternative to the more typical practice of simply leaving this task for your loved ones to do for you later. It may sound morbid, but it can be a liberating process. You are getting your house in order. You are getting things done—the way *you* want them done—while you still can. And you are lifting a painful and inevitable burden for the people you care about.

The philosophy behind Swedish Death Cleaning can apply to the way we live in other ways as well. For many years I have been inspired by the idea that, whether we're aware of it or not, each one of us has an essential mission in life. We all harbor a sense of purpose, unique purpose, and it is our life's work to figure out what that is and to achieve it. It's the question "What does 'done' look like?" writ large.

I recently had a conversation with a friend who feels the weight of this question acutely. She has had two strokes over the past couple of years. The second one was so severe, her doctors weren't sure she would survive it. But she did.

Now she is in a final encore. She knows she does not have long left on this earth. But she has two projects she is determined to complete. One is an autobiography. The other is an oral history of each of the pieces of her composed music. She wakes up every day with the intent and prayer that these things not be left unfinished when she dies. She is clear about what "done" looks like for her whole life. What if we could all give ourselves such a gift by approaching our life's goals as if they were a Swedish Death Cleaning project?

Chapter 7

START

The First Obvious Action

Today, Netflix is found in 183 million households worldwide. So it's almost hard to believe that it might not exist had Reed Hastings not been charged $40 by his local Blockbuster for losing the VHS tape of the Tom Hanks classic *Apollo 13*—prompting him to wonder if there might be a better way for people to borrow movies.

As a computer scientist who had studied at Stanford University in the 1980s, Hastings believed that within a decade or so the average household Internet connection would have the capacity to carry such massive amounts of data at such high speeds that entire movies could be instantly delivered on demand to one's personal computer or TV. Hastings's idea was to build Netflix as a DVD service first, "and then eventually the Internet would catch up with the postal system and pass it."

Hastings's ultimate vision for Netflix was a huge, complex undertaking, spanning many years and relying on technology that didn't yet exist. He could have started by laying out a multiyear, multiphase process. He could have made projections about when the speed of the Internet would surpass that of a FedEx truck hurtling down the highway, drafted multiple business plans for multiple scenarios, examined dozens or hundreds of variables such as the cost of shipping DVDs, the number of uses each disk can withstand, the losses the company could expect to take on unreturned or damaged DVDs, and so on.

Instead, Hastings mailed himself a single CD.

Hastings understood that unless DVDs could reliably be shipped through the mail and not get damaged or destroyed in transit the idea didn't have a chance. So he and his cofounder, Marc Randolph, went to a record store in Santa Cruz and bought a used CD. Then, Randolph recalls, they went to one of the little gift shop stores on Pacific Avenue and bought themselves "one of those little blue envelopes that you put the greeting cards in." They wrote Reed's home address on the envelope, stuck the CD inside, and mailed it with a single first-class stamp. "By the next day when he came to pick me up," Randolph says, "he had the envelope in his hand. It had arrived to his house with the un-broken CD in it. That was the moment where the two of us looked at each other and said, 'This idea just might work.' "

The concept was big—huge really. It was long term and ambitious. The cofounders knew what "done" looked like—the massive global streaming service and content library Netflix is today—but instead of mapping out a complex, detailed plan to get there, Hastings and Randolph looked for the ridiculously simple first step that would inform them whether they should take a second step or just walk away. Mailing that single disk turned out to be the simplest, most obvious way to set their immense idea in motion.

Take the Minimum Viable Action

You don't have to be overwhelmed by essential projects. Often, when you name the first obvious step, you avoid spending too much mental energy thinking about the fifth, seventh, or twenty-third steps. It doesn't matter if your project involves ten steps or a thousand. When you adopt this strategy, all you have to focus on is the very first step.

We often get overwhelmed because we misjudge what the first step is: what we think is the first step is actually several steps. But once we break that step down into concrete, physical actions, that first obvious action begins to feel effortless.

Productivity expert April Perry tells a story about a woman who needed help decluttering her living room. There were books everywhere: piles of books, boxes of books, books on top of the furniture, books covering just about every inch of surface, so many books that the room was barely usable. The woman knew that the solution to getting her books out of the living room was to buy bookshelves for her office. But even this seemingly simple solution felt overwhelming.

"If I brought you my computer right now," Perry asked her, "could you just open it and order bookshelves?"

"Well, I'd like to," she replied, "but first I need to measure my office walls and see which size I need to order."

"Okay," Perry said. "Could you go right now and measure your office walls?"

The woman replied that she could not, because she couldn't find her tape measure.

At this point they both started laughing. Suddenly it became clear that the real reason this woman hadn't made any progress was that she hadn't, until that moment, named the first obvious step: find, borrow, or buy a tape measure.

That first step may seem too trivial to name. But more often than not, a step as tiny as buying a tape measure provides the momentum we need to take the next step, then the next step after that.

I know many people who were inspired to try out Marie Kondo's world-famous method for tidying up their homes. They *loved* the idea of eliminating everything but the possessions that sparked joy for them. Unfortunately, some of them didn't get quite that far. That's because before you even get started, the Konmari Method requires you to "tidy your entire house all at once." The end state is, of course, desirable. But if the first step doesn't feel doable, many people will simply give up before they start.

An alternative is offered by Fumio Sasaki in *Goodbye, Things.* He suggests that the first action be "Discard something right now." He urges readers, "Don't wait till you have finished this book. The best way to go about it is to hone your skills as you part with your possessions. Why not close this book this very moment and discard something? . . . This is the first step, right now."

When I read that, I did just as Sasaki suggested: I stopped reading and discarded an old dried-up marker. It was so doable. And it felt good, so I spent ten more minutes discarding other things: old business cards, too-short pencils, a pile of magazines I knew I'd never read, a tangled mess of charging cables I'd stashed away "just in case I ever need them." In fact, while writing about this I was inspired to stop and discard the cardboard box that once held my not-so-new headphone set. And again I kept going, discarding even more things. Such is the power of taking the first, concrete, physical step: it ignites a subsequent surge of focused Effortless Action.

One key tenet of Silicon Valley thinking, and design thinking more generally, is the practice of building a *minimum viable product.* Eric Ries, author of *The Lean Startup,* defines a minimum viable product as "that version of a new product which allows a team to collect the maximum amount of validated learning about customers with the least amount of effort." It's an effortless way of testing an idea because it requires building only the simplest version of your product necessary to get reliable feedback about what your customers want.

Think of how the founders of Airbnb (then called AirBedAndBreakfast) famously tested their concept simply by posting a few photos of their apartment on a simple webpage. Soon they had three paying guests who wanted to stay there while they attended a design conference in the city. More important, they had what Ries calls "validated learning" that customers would actually want to use their product.

While this practice is disproportionately common in the start-up world, the same idea can be applied to any essential goal or project. Instead of procrastinating, wasting enormous amounts of time and effort planning for a million possible scenarios, or charging full steam ahead at the risk of traveling miles down the wrong path, we can opt for taking the minimum viable first action: the action that will allow us to gain the maximum learning from the least amount of effort.

This principle always reminds me of the line from Shakespeare's *A Midsummer Night's Dream,* "Though she be but little she is fierce." The first action may be the tiniest, easiest-to-overlook thing. But it is surprisingly fierce.

The Magic of Microbursts

A microburst is a meteorological surge that causes powerful winds and storms for a brief but intense period, often just ten to fifteen minutes. A column of wind drops from a rain cloud at speeds of up to sixty miles per hour, hitting the ground with such force that it can fell fully grown trees.

A microburst in April Perry's vernacular is a ten-minute surge of focused activity that can have an immediate effect on our essential project. It's the little burst of motivation and energy we get from taking that first obvious action. And from there your energy—and your confidence—only builds with every subsequent action. For example:

Essential Project	First Obvious Action	Microburst
Remove the clutter from the garage.	Find the broom.	Sweep out the shed and move the bikes into the shed.
Launch a product.	Open a cloud-based document to put ideas in.	Brainstorm product features.
Complete a large report.	Pick up a pen and a piece of paper.	Draft an outline for the report.

The Power of 2.5 Seconds

In recent years neuroscientists and psychologists have found that the "now" we experience lasts only 2.5 seconds. This is our psychological present. One of the implications of this is that progress can happen in tiny increments.

Two and a half seconds is enough time to shift our focus: to put the phone down, close the browser, take a deep breath. It's enough time to open a book, take out a blank sheet of paper, lace up our running shoes, or open up the junk drawer and fish out our tape measure.

Of course, 2.5 seconds is enough time to get caught up in nonessential activities too. The big tech companies understand this in their relentless competition for our attention. They are constantly testing new ways to offer us smaller units of information: 280 characters on Twitter, "likes" on Facebook and Instagram, newsfeeds we can scroll through and absorb at a glance. These bite-sized activities may not feel like wasting time—*after all,* we think, *what's a few seconds?* The trouble, of course, is that over time these activities rarely add up to making progress on the goals we hope to achieve. They are easy but pointless.

When we're struggling to name the first obvious action, we need to either make it a little easier to get started on what's important now or make it a little harder to do something trivial instead. Looking at that first step or action through the lens of 2.5 seconds is the change that makes every other change possible. It is the habit of habits.

Chapter 8

SIMPLIFY

Start with Zero

In February 1998, Peri Hartman left the four-story brick building at Second and Pike in Seattle, Washington, that served as Amazon's headquarters for a meeting with Jeff Bezos and Shel Kaphan, Amazon's first employee and the head of software development. He walked the block or so to a microbrewery located at the famed Pike Place Market, to talk with them over lunch.

Bezos had called the meeting because he'd been thinking a lot about the checkout process on his fast-growing e-commerce site—which at the time was riddled with friction. To place an order, customers had to go through a long series of steps, as was typical of online ordering at the time. There was a page to type in your name: click. A page to type in the first line of your address: click. City, zip code, type of credit card, credit card number, and expiration date. Adding a billing address was several more steps, with several pages: click, click, click. Shipping address: more clicks. There was no autofill function at the time, which meant it could take several minutes—or more—to complete a purchase.

At one point in the meal, Bezos said, "We need something to make the ordering system frictionless. We need to make it so the customer can order products with the least amount of effort. They should be able to click on one thing, and it's done."

Recalling the experience, Hartman says his marching orders were clear: "The goal was to make it easier." Bezos recognized that "the more steps there were, the more time they [the customer] had to change their mind. If you can get the user to buy it with one click they are more likely to make the purchase."

At the time, the whole idea of buying online was still new, and quite overwhelming for a lot of people. Navigating the long click-through process was not at all intuitive and was far more cumbersome than the process people were used to: that is, walking up to a counter and handing a store employee a credit card. To type in all of the billing, payment, and shipping info every time was a barrier, a hassle. Reducing all of that complexity to a single click was a huge breakthrough.

In hindsight, the one-click solution seemed obvious. Yet Hartman, an intelligent and passionate programmer, had at this point spent two to three months working on streamlining and simplifying each individual step of the checkout process and hadn't for a moment contemplated one-click ordering. "Nobody was doing it," he explained. "Jeff said let's do it. So we did it. "

Amazon filed a patent for the one-click process that lasted the better part of twenty years, giving them a huge advantage over online competitors. It's impossible to isolate the precise value of that single innovation, but it has, clearly, been enormous.

The Simplest Steps Are the Ones You Don't Take

It's striking to me that Hartman spent months trying to make each step in the online ordering process simpler but never thought to try *removing steps* to make *the process itself* simpler. There is a huge difference between the two.

No matter how simple the step, it's still easier to take no step.

When my son was twelve, he set a goal to become an Eagle Scout before he turned fourteen. It was a stretch-goal by any measure, but we tackled it together, making memories as we went.

Just before he turned fourteen, he began his final Eagle Project, which involved working with a team of forty people to rebuild a 180-foot-long fence that had been destroyed in the California fires the year before. Now all that remained was to finish a report about the project. It doesn't seem like much, but after almost two years of nonstop Scouts work, this one project seemed to expand in our minds until it became easier to put it off.

We got an early start on the project. In fact, by the time we lost momentum we were already about halfway through. But sometimes the second half of a project seems much more daunting than the first. We couldn't stop thinking of all kinds of extras that might make the report even better: an opening essay full of vivid and precise details, dozens of photos, professional-grade graphics. It didn't help that we had seen extravagant projects that other Scouts had spent hundreds of hours on (or, in most cases, that their parents had spent hundreds of hours on), which further raised the bar for the amount of effort we thought we needed to exert to get this done.

So the project stalled. Whenever we thought about picking it back up again, we felt overwhelmed. Days started to slip by with no progress being made.

After a couple of weeks of this, I happened to be researching process simplification in complex organizations. Suddenly I could see it: we were making this process so much more complicated than it had to be. By adding so many steps—even if just mentally—we were making it harder for ourselves to take any steps at all. So we took a step back and asked, "What are the minimum steps required to complete this?"

We didn't need to create a special wooden binder to put the report in. We didn't have to include every single photo we had taken. We didn't need to write up paragraph-length descriptions for each of the photos or design a fancy cover for the report. The opening essay didn't have to be a magnum opus.

Here is our pared-down list of truly essential steps: "Type up twenty phrases or quotes. Print them up. Cut them out. Stick them on. Print up something for the cover. Put in three section dividers. Write and print a three-page essay answering exactly, and only, the questions asked. Drive it to the Scouts office and drop it off." Done.

This important project for my son went from stalled to completed in a fraction of the time because we outlined and then completed the minimum number of steps. He became an Eagle Scout a week before he turned fourteen.

This concept, of course, is not unique to Eagle Scout projects. Universally, the single question that can save you untold headaches and get you moving on priority projects that seem overwhelmingly hard or complex is as follows:

What are the minimum steps required for completion?

To be clear, identifying the minimum number of steps is not the same as "phoning it in" or producing something you are not proud of. Unnecessary steps are just that: unnecessary. Eliminating them allows you to channel all your energy toward getting the important project done. In just about every realm, completion is infinitely better than adding superfluous steps that don't add value. And completion is something to be proud of:

In order to succeed at something, you have to get it done.

Not Everything Needs the Extra Mile

My best friend growing up consistently put in fewer hours of work than me but got better grades. His secret? When the teacher asked him to do something, he did what was asked and nothing more. That's it. I would go deep: I'd read beyond what I was asked to do, research more than was needed. I could get so busy going the second mile I wouldn't get the first mile done.

Going the extra mile in ways that are essential is one thing: a surgeon taking the extra step to prevent infection at the site of an incision, for example. But adding unnecessary, superficial embellishments is quite another. Here is a rule I have found helpful: *Being asked to do X isn't a good enough reason to do Y.*

For example, being asked to do a presentation isn't a good enough reason to create slides with videos and fancy graphics and pages upon pages of data. How often have you been forced to sit through a presentation with too many slides? Or too many words on each slide? Or too much of everything, period? Is that really the kind of experience you want to create for someone else?

A tiny but pivotal moment in IBM's legendary turnaround reveals a better approach. Lou Gerstner was new to his post as CEO and had invited Nick Donofrio, one of his executive leaders, to speak at a state-of-the-company meeting. Gerstner recalls, "At that time, the standard format of any important IBM meeting was a presentation using overhead projectors and graphics on transparencies that IBMers called—and no one remembers why—'foils.' Nick was on his second foil when I stepped to the table and, as politely as I could in front of his team, switched off the projector. After a long moment of awkward silence, I simply said, 'Let's just talk about your business.'"

That's what the goal for most presentations is supposed to be: to "just talk about your business." So the next time you have to write a report, give a presentation, or make a sales pitch, resist the temptation to add unnecessary extras. They aren't just a distraction for you; they're also a distraction for your audience. That's why, when I do presentations, I use six slides, with fewer than ten words total.

There is rarely a need to go that second mile beyond what's essential. It's better to go just the first mile than to not go anywhere at all.

Start with Zero

When a team of Apple's best product designers met with Steve Jobs to present their design for what eventually became the iDVD—a now-defunct application that allowed users to burn music, movies, and digital photo files stored on their computers onto a physical DVD—they expected their boss to be wowed. It was a beautiful, clean design, and while it had a number of features and functions, they were proud of how they had streamlined the original version of the product, which had required a thousand-page user manual.

But as the team soon learned, Jobs had something else in mind. He walked to the whiteboard and drew a rectangle. Then he said, "Here's the new application. It's got one window. You drag your video into the window. Then you click the button that says BURN. That's it. That's what we're going to make."

Mike Evangelist, one of the product designers in the meeting, was blown away. He said, "I still have the slides I prepared for that meeting, and they're ridiculous in their complexity." Only in retrospect could he clearly see that "all this other stuff was completely in the way."

Evangelist told me that his biggest "aha" was that he and his team had been looking at their *process* the wrong way. They had started with an immensely complicated product and attempted to pare it down. But Jobs came at it from the opposite angle. He started at zero and tried to figure out the absolute minimum number of steps required to achieve the desired outcome.

We've become so accustomed to the complexity of all the processes in our lives, we rarely stop to question it. For example, while writing this book, I launched a podcast. Originally, the instructions I was supposed to send to each guest who joined me on the podcast consisted of fifteen steps:

1. Log in to Zencastr.com using the following credentials:
2. Username: XYZ
3. Password: ABC
4. Click the link in the Zencastr email you receive shortly before the interview time.
5. To ensure best-quality audio, when prompted by Chrome, allow notifications from Zencastr.
6. Bookmark Zencastr (click the star icon on the right side of the URL bar in Chrome) as a failsafe to step 3.
7. Confirm that the mic Health Check says "Passed."
8. If it doesn't, click the tab at the bottom center of the soundbar rectangle with your name to see what the issue is, click the link and troubleshoot.
9. Confirm you can hear me and we can speak to each other via Zencastr.

10. Click the Zoom link I email to you (it should also be in the calendar invite).
11. Once it lets you into the Zoom video, immediately mute the Zoom microphone.
12. Enable video on Zoom.
13. Once I hit recording on both Zencastr and Zoom, confirm that you can see the recording icons on both and perform a clap test with me.
14. Then we will get started!
15. Once completed, please Log Out of Zencastr before you close the window.

This was overwhelming for me even to *read*, never mind for guests to actually follow and do.

So I started from zero. I asked myself, "What is the minimum number of steps someone could take to chat with me via Zencastr?" Once I had my answer, I reduced the process to this:

1. Click the link in the Zencastr email you receive shortly before the interview.
2. I'll start and end the recording so all you need to do is chat.

That was it. Just two easy steps. If there are processes in your life that seem to involve an inordinate number of steps, try starting from zero. Then see if you can find your way back to those same results, only take fewer steps.

Maximize the Steps Not Taken

In February 2001, seventeen independent-minded people met at the Lodge at Snowbird (a ski resort in Utah, up in the Wasatch Mountains) to relax, talk, eat, ski, and discuss software. What came out of their conversations that weekend was a now widely read document called the "Manifesto for Agile Software Development." In it, they codified a set of principles for developing better software by removing obstacles and friction to create an effortless user experience.

One of the twelve principles of the Agile Manifesto states, "Simplicity—the art of maximizing the amount of work not done—is essential." By this they mean that the goal is to create value for the customer, and if this can be done with less code and fewer features, that is exactly what ought to be done.

While this principle refers to the process of software development, we can adapt it to any everyday process by saying, "Simplicity—the art of maximizing *the steps not taken*—is essential." In other words, regardless of what our ultimate goal is, we should focus on only those steps that add value. Every nonessential step comes with an opportunity cost, so for each nonessential step removed, we gain more time, energy, and cognitive resources to put toward what's essential.

You might be surprised at how many seemingly complex goals can be obtained, and how many seemingly complex tasks can be completed, in just a few steps. As sportswriter Andy Benoit observes, most geniuses "prosper not by deconstructing intricate complexities but by exploiting unrecognized simplicities."

CHAPTER 9

PROGRESS

The Courage to Be Rubbish

In 1959 a British industrialist named Henry Kremer had a dream of a future where human-powered flight was possible for the masses. Determined to do anything he could to make that dream a reality, he launched the Kremer Prize: generous rewards meant to incentivize designers to build aircraft that could be powered entirely by a single person.

One prize, for £50,000, would go to the first team to create an aircraft that could fly a figure eight around two pylons, half a mile apart. Another prize, for £100,000, was also offered, for the first team to fly an aircraft across the English Channel.

Given the aeronautical achievements of the time, constructing what amounted to a workable flying bicycle seemed like a realistic challenge. It was, after all, a full half century after Orville Wright had made his flight south of Kitty Hawk in North Carolina and forty years since the first nonstop transatlantic flight. A full decade before, Chuck Yeager had broken the sound barrier. And just a decade later, Neil Armstrong and Buzz Aldrin would walk on the moon. But however doable the challenge might have seemed, many talented teams had tried and failed—for over seventeen years.

Enter Paul MacCready. Saddled with a huge debt at the time, he didn't have a team at all—save for friends and family, including his young son, whom he enlisted as his test pilot. Meanwhile, his competitors were all well staffed and well funded and built "big, complex, elegant airplanes" with large-span wings, many wooden "ribs," and metal or heavy plastic casings. Yet these teams "didn't come close to achieving" the prize.

At first, MacCready couldn't figure out why. Then it hit him: everyone had been working to solve the wrong problem. The real challenge wasn't to build an elegant aircraft that could do the figure eight on the field around the two pylons; it was to build a large, light aircraft, "no matter how ugly it is," that you could crash, "then repair, modify, alter, redesign—fast." That was when he suddenly realized, "There is an easy way to do it."

So MacCready and his son immediately got to work on a model, inspired by one of the simplest and most aerodynamic mechanisms in nature: bird flight. Within two months they were flying the first version of the *Gossamer Condor.* It weighed just fifty-five pounds (twenty-five kilos) and looked amateurish, especially compared to the sleeker models others had created, but that was exactly the point. MacCready said, "If it crashed on landing you'd get a broom handle and duct tape and tape the broom handle back on and you'd be back flying in five minutes. That accident would have kept those [other larger, more sophisticated teams] from flying for something like six months. So we got a huge amount of flight experience out of this."

Over the course of just a few months, the *Gossamer Condor* made some 222 flights—sometimes several in a single day. Some of his competitors' machines didn't achieve that in their lifetimes.

It was on its 223rd flight that the *Condor* completed the figure eight challenge and won the first Kremer Prize. Two years later MacCready would win the second Kremer Prize when the *Gossamer Albatross* successfully crossed the English Channel.

His most brilliant insight wasn't some advanced breakthrough in the science of flight. It was simply that focusing on the elegance and sophistication of the aircraft was actually an impediment to progress. An ugly aircraft that could be crashed, repaired, and redesigned fast would make it much easier to make progress on what really mattered: building a plane that could, as MacCready put it, "turn left, turn right, go up high enough [at] the beginning and the end of the flight."

Similarly, in your own pursuit of what matters, if you want to "build a better airplane," don't try to get everything exactly right the first time. Instead, embrace the rubbish "no matter how ugly it is" so you can crash, repair, modify, and redesign fast. It's a far easier path for learning, growing, and making progress on what's essential.

Start with Rubbish

Many of us are kept back from producing something wonderful because we misunderstand the creative process. We see something exceptional or beautiful in its finished state and we imagine it started out as a beautiful, Baby Yoda version of what we are looking at. But exactly the opposite is true.

Ed Catmull, the former CEO of Pixar, once said, "We all start out ugly. Every one of Pixar's stories starts out that way." Their earliest sketches are, according to Catmull, "awkward and unformed, vulnerable and incomplete." This is why Catmull has always worked hard to foster a culture that creates space for such "rubbish": because he understands there would be no Buzz Lightyear without hundreds of awful ideas along the way. As he puts it, "Pixar is set up to protect our director's ugly baby."

At the pharmaceutical company Pfizer, they use a program called "Dare to Try" that emphasizes seven specific behaviors to foster innovation. For example, "freshness" encourages employees to find ideas in new places, "playfulness" taps into childlike curiosity and fun, and "greenhousing" protects their early ideas, no matter how rubbish, from harsh criticism so that they are allowed to grow.

Overachievers tend to struggle with the notion of starting with rubbish; they hold themselves to a high standard of perfection at every stage in the process. But the standard to which they hold themselves is neither realistic nor productive.

For example, many people cite learning a new language as an essential project, a dream that matters to them. But they never practice because they are embarrassed. They want to be flawless—or at least not make fools of themselves—from the start. But a friend of mine who teaches Spanish sees it differently. As an exceptional student himself (with a JD from Stanford Law School followed by a doctorate from Princeton as well), he has learned that when it comes to languages, embracing mistakes leads to accelerated learning. He teaches his language students to imagine they have a bag full of one thousand beads. Every time they make a mistake talking to someone else in the language they take out one bead. When the bag is empty they will have achieved level 1 mastery. The faster they make those mistakes, the faster they will progress.

Is there something new you want to learn but feel overwhelmed by? Something that you know would add great value to you either personally or professionally but that you feel intimidated by because of the long road to mastery? Then try your own version of the "bag of beads" exercise and shift your focus to making as many mistakes as possible when you're starting out.

There is no mastery without mistakes. And there is no learning later without the courage to be rubbish.

I, for example, recently decided to take a class online. One approach to passing this class might have been to read through the mountains of lecture materials carefully and thoroughly, watch all of the videos, take detailed notes, and memorize everything, with the goal of getting 100 percent on every practice quiz, every time. However, such an approach sounds like extremely hard work. The likely outcome would be acing the first quiz or two before burning out, abandoning the effort, and never making it to the exam. Instead, I decided to simply take the quiz without any preparation, knowing I would get roughly 50 percent of the answers wrong. That was in fact my goal: to get them wrong as quickly as possible so I could see the correct answers. I didn't want to waste time and energy on what I already knew; I wanted to see what I didn't know so I could focus only on that. At first, I got rubbish scores on quite a few practice tests. Then I'd look at what I got wrong and take more practice tests. Pretty soon my scores were less rubbish, and then even less rubbish. Eventually I'll have what I need to pass the test.

Make Failure as Cheap as Possible

Giving ourselves permission to fail takes courage. It feels scary. It makes us vulnerable. The higher the stakes, the more courage is required. So given that our reserves of courage are limited, we want to find ways to experience—and learn from—failure as cheaply as possible.

For example, when our children were younger, Anna and I wanted them to have the chance to be rubbish with money while the stakes were low. After all, we'd much rather they made mistakes with their allowance at the ages of eight and ten than make mistakes with their life savings as adults. So we gave them three glass jars: one for charity, one for saving, and one for spending. When they received their allowance, it was up to them to divide up the money. We didn't try to advise them on how much should go to saving or spending. We wanted *them* to make the decisions, especially the rubbish ones. For example, our son once spent $40 he'd saved on an electric racing car, and he regretted it afterward. He wished he had that money for a major LEGO purchase he was saving up for. Now he is a teenager and is saving up for a major service mission he wants to go on that will cost thousands of dollars, and I am confident he won't regret it. That's because he got to learn from his mistakes while the risks were lower. I call these kinds of mistakes learning-sized mistakes. We don't want our children to learn about money the hard way; we want them to learn about it the easy way, the cheaper way.

To make effortless progress on what matters, learning-sized mistakes must be encouraged. This isn't giving yourself—or others—permission to consistently produce poor-quality work; it's simply letting go of the absurd pressure to always do everything perfectly. As Reid Hoffman, one of the PayPal Mafia and cofounder of LinkedIn, once told Ben Casnocha, his newly hired chief of staff, "In order to move fast, I expect you'll make some foot faults. I'm okay with an error rate of 10–20% . . . if it means you can move fast." Ben recalls, "I felt empowered to make decisions with this ratio in mind, and it was incredibly liberating."

Not surprisingly, Reid also advocates the same philosophy in entrepreneurship and business. "If you're not embarrassed by your first product release," he says, "you released it too late." Or put another way, "When it comes to product launches, imperfect is perfect."

Protect Your Rubbish from the Harsh Critic in Your Head

Another way we can make failure as cheap as possible for ourselves is simply to protect our rubbish from the harsh critic in our heads. Instead of shaming yourself for hitting your serve into the net, celebrate the fact that you're on the court to begin with. Instead of belittling yourself for even the tiniest of errors, be proud of the fact that you are unlikely to make that same mistake ever again. Any time you feel like you're on shaky ground with some meaningful challenge you've taken on, talk to yourself like you would talk to a toddler learning to walk: "You've taken the first step. You may feel wobbly now, but you've begun. You're going to get there."

And remind yourself that every great achievement is rubbish at the beginning. Every one of them. As the Irish playwright George Bernard Shaw once said, "A life spent in making mistakes is not only more honorable but more useful than a life spent doing nothing."

Adopt a "Zero-Draft" Approach

I have met many people who feel a calling to write a book. But they often give up before writing even the first draft of the first chapter. Their belief that each sentence has to be perfect—or close to perfect—to be worthy of the page keeps them from even starting the process. I recommend they adopt a "zero-draft" approach. That is, write a version of that first chapter that's so rough it wouldn't even qualify as a first draft.

The idea with the zero draft is to write *anything*. The more rubbish the better. It doesn't have to be seen by anyone. It never has to be judged. Don't even think of it as a draft; it's just words on a page. You'd be surprised how easy it is to get your creative juices flowing this way. As American poet and memoirist Maya Angelou put it, “When I am writing, I write. And then it’s as if the muse is convinced I’m serious and says ‘Okay. Okay. I’ll come.’ ”

Margaret Atwood, the prolific author of eighteen books of poetry, eighteen novels, eleven books of nonfiction, nine collections of short fiction, and eight children’s books, once wrote, “A word after a word after a word is power.” Even rubbish words are more powerful than a blank page. In fact, they are much more powerful, because there can be no magnum opus later without those rubbish words now.

So if you are feeling overwhelmed by an essential project because you think you have to produce something flawless from the outset, simply lower the bar to start. Whether it’s writing a book, composing a song, painting a canvas, or any other creative pursuit that calls to you, inspiration flows from the courage to start with rubbish.

By embracing imperfection, by having the courage to be rubbish, we can begin. And once we begin, we become a little less rubbish, and then a little less. And eventually, out of the rubbish come exceptional, effortless breakthroughs in the things that matter.

Chapter 10

PACE

Slow Is Smooth, Smooth Is Fast

In the midst of the great age of exploration, in the early years of the twentieth century, the most sought-after goal in the world was to reach the South Pole. It had never been done before in all of recorded human history: not by Pytheas, the first polar explorer circa 320 B.C.E., not by the Vikings a thousand years later, not by the Royal Navy in all its prowess during the years of the great British Empire.

In November 1911 two "rivals for the pole" aimed to be the first to achieve this elusive goal: Captain Robert Falcon Scott from Great Britain, and Roald Amundsen from Norway, otherwise known as "the Last Viking."

They began within days of each other a 1,500-mile race against time, a race of life and death. One team would return victorious; the other would not return.

To read their journals, however, you would never guess that the two teams made the exact same journey, under the exact same conditions. On the good weather days, Scott would drive his team to exhaustion. On bad weather days he would hunker down in his tent and lodge his complaints in his journal. On one such day he wrote, "Our luck in weather is preposterous. It makes me feel a little bitter to contrast such weather with that experienced by our predecessors." On another, he wrote, "I doubt if any party could travel in such weather."

But one party could. On a day of a similar blizzard, Amundsen recorded in his journal, "It has been an unpleasant day—storm, drift, and frostbite, but we have advanced 13 miles closer to our goal."

On December 12, 1911, the plot thickened: Amundsen and his team got within forty-five miles of the South Pole, closer than anyone who had ever tried before. They had traveled some 650 grueling miles and were on the verge of winning the race of their lives. And the icing on the cake: the weather that day was working in their favor. Amundsen wrote, "Going and surface as good as ever. Weather splendid—calm with sunshine." There on the Polar Plateau, they had the ideal conditions to ski and sled their way to the South Pole. With one big push, they could be there in a single day.

Instead, it took three days. Why?

From the very start of their journey, Amundsen had insisted that his party advance exactly fifteen miles each day—no more, and no less. The final leg would be no different. Rain or shine, Amundsen "would not allow the daily 15 miles to be exceeded." While Scott allowed his team to rest only on the days "when it froze" and pushed his team to the point of "inhuman exertion" on the days "when it thawed," Amundsen "insisted on plenty of rest" and kept a steady pace for the duration of the trip to the South Pole.

This one simple difference between their approaches can explain why Amundsen's team made it to the top while Scott's team perished. Setting a steady, consistent, sustainable pace was ultimately what allowed the party from Norway to reach their destination "without particular effort," as Roland Hunford, the author of a fascinating book on this race to the South Pole, explains.

Without particular effort? They accomplished a feat that had eluded adventurers for millennia. Of course, not every day was easy. But even under the harshest of conditions, the goal was doable, thanks to that one simple rule: they would not exceed fifteen miles a day, no matter what.

On December 14, 1911, Amundsen led his team to become the first in recorded history to reach the South Pole. And then they safely made the sixteen-thousand-mile journey home. Meanwhile, Scott and his exhausted, demoralized team arrived at the pole only to find they were some thirty-four days too late. Their return journey was even more wretched; the team staggered on in total exhaustion, frostbite taking its ghastly toll until all five men froze to death. Some of them were so certain this would be their fate, they wrote notes they hoped their friends and families would one day read.

The False Economy of Powering Through

When we try to make too much progress on a goal or project right out of the gate, we can get trapped in a vicious cycle: we get tired, so then we take a break, but then we think we have to make up for the time lost, so we sprint again. For example, I had a friend who was desperate to finish writing her business plan. So one weekend, she decided to spend every waking minute on it. She powered through. But it burned her out to the point that she couldn't bear to think about the plan, much less work on it again for weeks. She said, "When I tried, my brain just shut down."

As a teenager I set a goal to compete in a three-mile, cross-country race where I grew up in Yorkshire, England. When the day arrived, I was nervous. With my parents and grandparents looking on, I made my way to the starting line. Even though I didn't feel fully prepared, I could have done okay if I had started out the way I had intended: slowly. I liked to run that way: to start slow and gradually pick up speed, feeling the rush of adrenaline as I passed other runners from behind. But my nerves got the better of me. I threw out my game plan and shot out of the gate along with the other runners. I sprinted, hard, for the first hundred yards, then had to pause, gasping for breath, just one hundred yards in. Eventually I caught my breath, but the damage had been done: I'd fallen behind, and I remained behind the whole time. It was painful. I came in fifty-seventh place out of sixty runners. In hindsight, the cost of that sprint was more than the loss of just one race. The loss was humiliating enough that I never again competed in any other cross-country meets.

When we're trying to achieve something that matters to us, it's tempting to want to sprint out of the gate. The problem is that going too fast at the beginning will almost always slow us down the rest of the way.

The costs of this boom-and-bust approach to getting important projects done is too high: we feel exhausted on the days we sprint hard, drained and demoralized on the days we don't, and more often than not we wind up like those British explorers, feeling battered and broken and still no closer to achieving our goal.

Luckily, there is an alternative. We can find the effortless pace.

The Upside of Upper Bounds

In my early days as an aspiring author I was passionate and motivated, but inconsistent. I would write some days. I'd talk about writing on other days. And I'd talk about what I was thinking about writing on other days in between. Meanwhile, I had a musician friend who decided to write a book about her songs. She was prolific in how much music she had produced: she had written over 3,000 songs, 101 albums, and 9 cantatas. Her music had been featured around the world, including at National Prayer Breakfasts, at a presidential inauguration, and on *The Oprah Winfrey Show.* It was breathtaking to see all that she'd accomplished at her steady pace over many years. But how would she fare as a writer?

Quite well, as it turned out. She decided she would choose one hundred songs and tell the story behind each of them. She would write two stories a week, "so it was manageable," she explained. And when those two stories were finished, she would stop work for the week, even if she had the energy and appetite to write more. Two stories a week was her upper bound. I was stunned to learn that within nine months her book was finished and sent to the publisher. Meanwhile, I was still working on mine intermittently.

Holding back when you still have steam in you might seem like a counterintuitive approach to getting important things done, but in fact, this kind of restraint is key to breakthrough productivity. As Lisa Jewell, author of some eighteen bestselling novels, put it, "Pace yourself. If you write too much, too quickly, you'll go off at tangents and lose your way and if you write infrequently you'll lose your momentum. A thousand words a day is a good ticking over amount."

Ben Bergeron is a former Ironman triathlete who trains the fittest athletes in the United Kingdom. Clearly, he is not lacking in the physical stamina to work extra hours when a client requires it, but he has a rule that keeps him performing well professionally and personally: he leaves the office at 5:25 P.M. every single day. On a slow day, he leaves the office at 5:25 P.M. On a busy day? He leaves the office at 5:25 P.M. It's nonnegotiable. Even if he is in a meeting, as soon as the clock strikes 5:25 P.M., he just stands up and walks to the door. He doesn't have to think about it. By now, everyone he works with knows that no rudeness is intended. It's simply that his upper bound is 5:25 P.M.

Whether it's "miles per day" or "words per day" or "hours per day," there are few better ways to achieve effortless pace than to set an upper bound.

The Right Range

All of us want to achieve our desired outcomes (complete the manuscript, run the 5K, launch the product) as quickly as possible. So it makes sense that we all prefer days when we make more progress than less. After all, few things in life are as satisfying as the feeling of accomplishment. But in our overenthusiasm for getting things done, we may make the mistake of thinking that all progress is created equal.

All progress is not created equal.

One of our daughters learned this the hard way when we made her responsible for taking care of the chickens (yes, we have chickens). This included collecting their eggs, feeding them, and refilling their water. We encouraged her to do so every day. But she reasoned that skipping the chore for a few days and then doing more every third day was really the same thing. After all, she argued, she could just collect three times more eggs, and leave three times more food and water all at once. But then there was an unexpected change in the weather: it turned hot. This meant that the chickens drank more water than usual *and* the remaining water evaporated more quickly than normal. Our daughter was devastated when she informed us that one of our chickens had died in the heat because they ran out of water.

So much in life is out of our control. The weather is out of our control. Wildfires, hurricanes, and new strains of coronaviruses are out of our control. Our kid getting a cold, the car breaking down, a friend going through a hard time who needs our counsel—how can we maintain a steady pace when any number of unexpected crises could pop up and throw us off schedule?

Since the end of the Cold War, the military has used the acronym VUCA to describe our global environment: one that is volatile, uncertain, complex, and ambiguous. In response to this new normal, the military has developed several approaches we can apply to make it easier to do what matters on our own everyday battlegrounds.

One is captured in the military mantra "Slow is smooth. Smooth is fast"—meaning, when you go slow, things are smoother, and when things are smooth, you can move faster. This is particularly true in conflicts where the ability to move in a coordinated fashion while staying alert to possible threats from every direction—and often while carrying weapons—is key. If you stop or move too slowly, you become an easy target. "But if you move too fast, you get surrounded and outflanked," as consultant Joe Indvik writes.

Indvik continues, "If you look closely at how elite infantry move, it looks like this: somewhere between a walk and a run, underscored by quick but careful footfalls, with weapons raised while rhythmically scanning the battlefield in all directions."

Less experienced infantry, he says, "will often zealously sprint into battle and give the impression of momentum." The problem with this approach is that as soon as they are in danger they will have to sprint to take cover at the first chance they get, and may end up in a place they haven't had time to survey or assess. . . . "Like the proverbial hare, this cycle of sprint-and-recover may seem fast in the moment, but long-term progress through the environment is slow and plagued by unidentified threats."

When you go slow, things are smoother. You have time to observe, to plan, to coordinate efforts. But go *too* slow and you may get stuck or lose your momentum. This is just as true in life and work as it is on the battlefield. To make progress despite the complexity and uncertainty we encounter on a daily basis, we need to choose the right range and keep within it.

Even when we want to make consistent, steady progress on a priority project, life often intervenes. We may have planned to spend the morning at our desk and instead find ourselves stuck in meetings. We may have blocked off hours on our calendar for important work and instead find ourselves dealing with a toddler meltdown. Then to compensate for our perceived lack of productivity, we work all the way through the weekend, in a mad rush for progress. We know this comes at a cost: low-quality work, increased guilt, and reduced confidence.

There's an easier alternative. We can establish upper and lower bounds. Simply use the following rule: Never less than X, never more than Y.

Essential Project	Lower Bound	Upper Bound
Finish reading *Les Misérables* in six months	Never less than five pages a day	Never more than twenty-five pages a day
Hit my sales numbers for the month	Never less than five sales calls a day	Never more than ten sales calls a day
Call my family every week for a month	Never talk for less than five minutes	Never talk for more than an hour
Complete an online class	Never less than signing in to the class every day	Never more than fifty minutes taking one practice test each day
Complete the first draft of a book	Never less than five hundred words a day	Never more than one thousand words a day

Finding the right range keeps us moving at a steady pace so we can make consistent progress. The lower bound should be high enough to keep us feeling motivated, and low enough that we can still achieve it even on days when we're dealing with unexpected chaos. The upper bound should be high enough to constitute good progress, but not so high as to leave us feeling exhausted. Once we get into the rhythm, the progress begins to flow. We are able to take Effortless Action.

An Effortless Summary

Part I	Effortless State
What is the Effortless State?	The Effortless State is an experience many of us have had when we are physically rested, emotionally unburdened, and mentally energized. You are completely aware, alert, present, attentive, and focused on what's important in this moment. You are able to focus on what matters most with ease.
INVERT	Instead of asking, "Why is this so hard?," invert the question by asking, "What if this could be easy?" Challenge the assumption that the "right" way is, inevitably, the harder one. Make the impossible possible by finding an indirect approach. When faced with work that feels overwhelming, ask, "How am I making this harder than it needs to be?"
ENJOY	Pair the most essential activities with the most enjoyable ones. Accept that work and play can co-exist. Turn tedious tasks into meaningful rituals. Allow laughter and fun to lighten more of your moments.
RELEASE	Let go of emotional burdens you don't need to keep carrying. Remember: When you focus on what you lack, you lose what you have. When you focus on what you have, you get what you lack. Use this habit recipe: "Each time I complain I will say something I am thankful for." Relieve a grudge of its duties by asking, "What job have I hired this grudge to do?"

REST	Discover the art of doing nothing. Do not do more today than you can completely recover from by tomorrow. Break down essential work into three sessions of no more than ninety minutes each. Take an effortless nap.
NOTICE	Achieve a state of heightened awareness by harnessing the power of presence. Train your brain to focus on the important and ignore the irrelevant. To see others more clearly, set aside your opinions, advice, and judgment, and put their truth above your own. Clear the clutter in your physical environment before clearing the clutter in your mind.
Part II	**Effortless Action**
What is Effortless Action?	Effortless Action means accomplishing more by trying less. You stop procrastinating and take the first obvious step. You arrive at the point of completion without overthinking and overthinking. You make progress by pacing yourself rather than powering through. You overachieve without overexerting.
DEFINE	To get started on an essential project, first define what "done" looks like. Establish clear conditions for completion, get there, then stop. Take sixty seconds to focus on your desired outcome. Write a "Done for the Day" list. Limit it to items that would constitute meaningful progress.
START	Make the first action the most obvious one. Break the first obvious action down into the tiniest, concrete step. Then name it. Gain maximum learning from minimal viable effort. Start with a ten-minute microburst of focused activity to boost motivation and energy.

SIMPLIFY	To simplify the process, don't simplify the steps: simply remove them. Recognize that not everything requires you to go the extra mile. Maximize the steps not taken. Measure progress in the tiniest of increments.
PROGRESS	When you start a project, start with rubbish. Adopt a "zero-draft" approach and just put some words, any words, on the page. Fail cheaply: make learning-sized mistakes. Protect your progress from the harsh critic in your head.
PACE	Set an effortless pace: slow is smooth, smooth is fast. Reject the false economy of "powering through." Create the right range: *I will never do less than X, never more than Y.* Recognize that not all progress is created equal.

effortless results

PART III

Steve Nash still holds the record for career free-throw percentage in the NBA. When he retired, his record was 90.43. The average for elite players is between 70 and 75 percent.

How did he do it? One reporter who interviewed Nash several years following his retirement described it this way: "Watching him shoot is akin to watching a stunningly elaborate automaton at work, his body moving with an exactness more reminiscent of clockwork than a fallible human being. At one point in our afternoon together, he homes in so precisely on his target that he stops having to move to retrieve the ball; instead, time after time, it descends through the rim in such a way that the *fwip* of the net sends it bouncing back to him, as if by magnetic force."

This is what it means to achieve *Effortless Results:* not to achieve a result once through intense effort, but to effortlessly achieve a result again and again.

What do I mean? Whenever your inputs create a one-time output you are getting a linear result. Every day you start from zero. If you don't put in the effort today, then you don't get the result today. It's a one-to-one ratio: the amount of effort you put in equals the results received. Linear results exist in every area of endeavor. For example:

An employee who works an hour and gets paid for that hour has a linear income.

A student who crams for a test, regurgitates facts, and gets a grade is acquiring linear knowledge.

A person who decides to exercise for an hour today but tomorrow has to decide again whether to exercise has made a linear decision.

An entrepreneur who makes money only when she is actively working to make it happen has a linear business model.

A volunteer who serves once and makes an impact once has made a linear contribution.

A person who exerts great effort to "make herself" do something today takes linear action.

A father who has to remind his children to do the same chore every day is practicing linear parenting.

Linear results are limited: they can never exceed the amount of effort exerted. What many people don't realize, however, is that there exists a far better alternative.

Residual results are completely different. With residual results you exert effort once and reap the benefits again and again. Results continue to flow to you, whether you put in additional effort or not. Results flow to you while you are sleeping. Results flow to you when you are taking the day off. Residual results can be virtually infinite. For example:

An author who writes a book and is paid royalties for years is getting residual income.

A student who learns first principles and can then apply that understanding in a variety of ways over time is acquiring residual knowledge.

A person who makes the one-time decision to exercise every day has made a residual decision.

An entrepreneur who sets up her business to work even when she is on vacation for six months has a residual business.
A social entrepreneur who provides microloans that are repaid so they can be loaned out again and again is making a residual contribution.
A person who does something every day, habitually, without thinking, without effort, is benefiting from residual action.
A mother who delegates a whole chore to her child and makes it fun, so it happens every day without prodding, is practicing residual parenting.

Does it sound like I'm exaggerating? I'm not. The thought of getting perpetual results might seem improbable if you are used to taking one action and getting one result. But there are tools we can use to turn our modest effort into Effortless Results, again and again.

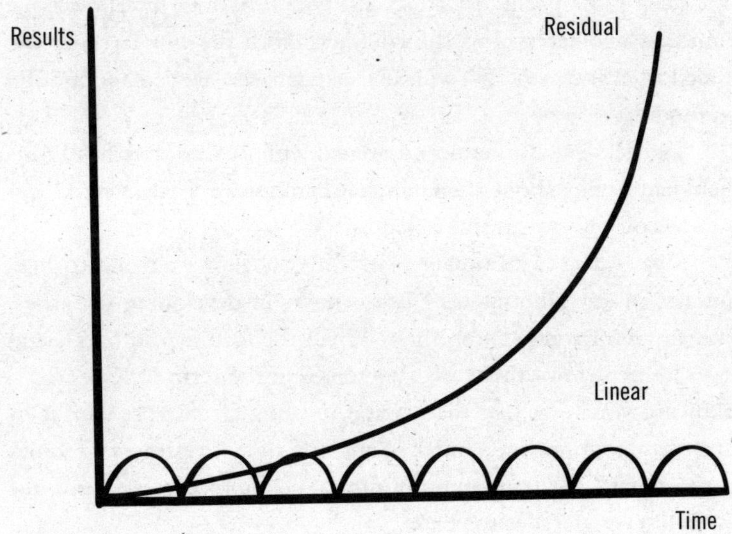

Residual results are like compound interest. Benjamin Franklin summarized the idea of compounding interest best when he said, "Money makes money. And the money that money makes, makes money." Put another way, when we are generating compound interest, we are creating effortless wealth.

This principle can be applied to many other pursuits as well.

The Case for Compounding Results

For example, a friend of mine, Jessica Jackley, was once doing voluntary service in East Africa when she met a local fishmonger named Katherine.

There was a great demand for fish in Katherine's village. Each day, she purchased about a half-dozen fish at a time from a middleman and then resold them at a roadside stand. But with seven children to feed, she wished she could buy directly from the fisherman and keep more profit. To do so, she would have to travel over one hundred kilometers, but she couldn't afford the bus fare—or the time lost at the market. To make it happen, she needed about $500 in funding.

Villagers like Katherine, combined with a recent talk from Muhammad Yunus about the Grameen Bank, were what inspired Jessica to cofound a platform called Kiva.

Kiva is a crowdsourcing platform that allows anyone to loan money, in any amount, to entrepreneurs in developing countries. But the returns don't stop there. When the loan is paid back—and over 98 percent of them are—it's repaid in the form of Kiva credit, allowing you to reloan that capital to another entrepreneur. This cycle can continue indefinitely. Your one-time investment becomes a perpetual fund that supports more and more entrepreneurs for years or even decades to come.

Instead of simply giving Katherine a one-time gift of $500, Jessica built a platform that has distributed over $1.3 billion in loans. That's the difference between linear and residual results.

Powerless Effort Versus Effortless Power

A lever is a simple machine that makes work easier. It's made up of a rigid beam that rests on top of a fulcrum. The longer the distance between the fulcrum and the spot on the beam where force is exerted, the less force is required to move a heavy object or lift a heavy load. The lever, in other words, multiplies the impact of the effort we put in. Whenever you have played on a seesaw, used a bottle opener or crowbar, or rowed a boat, you were using a lever.

Archimedes, the Greek mathematician and mechanical engineer, is considered the first to have discovered the principle of leverage. He is thought to have said that if he had a long enough lever and the right place to stand, he could move the world. I am fascinated by how we can apply the principle of leverage in other areas. Here are a few (of many) examples:

Lever	Modest Input, Residual Results
Learning	Personal capability compounds over time. You develop a reputation once, but then opportunities flow to you for years. You understand first principles deeply and then can easily apply them again and again. You establish a habit once, but then it serves you for a lifetime.
Teaching	Sharing knowledge is powerful. Teach others to teach, and you get exponential impact. You craft the right story once, and it can live on for millennia. The more we teach, the more we ourselves learn.

Lever	Modest Input, Residual Results
Automating	Automate something once, and then forget about it as it continues to work perpetually. Write up a cheat sheet once, and use it every day afterward. Write lines of code, or hire someone to write them, and then they will perform the same actions thousands of times. You can write a book once, but then millions can read it even hundreds of years later.
Trusting	If you hire the right person once, they'll produce results hundreds of times. When you reduce friction on or across teams up front, collaboration flows smoothly on project after project. When you build a unified team where everybody knows who is doing what, it becomes easier to stay aligned on roles, responsibilities, regulations, rewards, and desired results.
Preventing	Solving a problem before it happens can save you endless time and aggravation later on. Strike a problem at its roots, and you can prevent it from resurfacing again and again. Preventing a crisis now is always easier than managing it in the future.

Of course, there can be drawbacks to levers too. Depending on which lever you push, an equally modest amount of effort can also produce amazingly *bad* residual results. A bad reputation can cost you opportunities for years. A bad habit can compromise your health for decades. Hire the wrong person, and they can negatively affect your business in a hundred ways. Write bad code, and users will be frustrated again and again. The direction the force will flow is entirely up to us.

There are two ways to approach getting things done: the hard way is with powerless effort, and the easy way is with effortless power. Levers give us effortless power. The next few chapters will show how to use this powerful tool to produce the right results.

CHAPTER 11

LEARN

Leverage the Best of What Others Know

The year 1642 began with the death of Galileo Galilei, the father of observational astronomy. It ended with the premature birth of Isaac Newton on Christmas Day. Born weighing just three pounds, Newton was described by his mother as "small enough to fit in a quart pot." He was expected to live only a few days. Instead, he went on to study at Trinity College, Cambridge, and to author what became known as *Philosophiae Naturalis Principia Mathematica,* or often just *Principia* for short. Among other contributions, this extraordinary document codified the three laws of motion as well as the law of universal gravitation: the principles that form the foundation of the entire field of physics.

These principles explained how physical objects moved through the world. They described the motion of planets in our solar system. They were critical in fueling the scientific revolution and the industrial revolutions that followed. It is no exaggeration to say that they changed the world. Without them, we couldn't have built the automobile, invented the jet plane, or put a man on the moon.

Of course, Newton's writings didn't offer step-by-step instructions for how to build an automotive engine, a jet plane, or a spacecraft. Instead, they offered something far more valuable: a set of *principles* that could later be applied to automotive engineering, aeronautics, space travel, and more.

As our lives become increasingly busy, overwhelming, and fast-paced, it's tempting to seek out easy instructions or methods that we can apply to a problem right away, without expending much mental energy. This is a mistake. Why? A method may be useful once, to solve one specific type of problem. Principles, however, can be applied broadly and repeatedly. At their best, they are universal and timeless.

Specific methods, in other words, produce only linear results. If it's residual results we're after, we must look to principles. In fact, the word *principia* means "first principles, fundamental beginnings or elements." First principles are like the building blocks of knowledge: once you understand them correctly you can apply them hundreds of times.

Harrington Emerson, the American efficiency engineer known for his pioneering contributions to the field of management, once said, "As to methods, there may be a million and then some, but principles are few. The man who grasps principles can successfully select his own methods. The man who tries methods, ignoring principles, is sure to have trouble."

Seek Principles

Not all knowledge has lasting value.

Some knowledge is useful just once. For example, you memorize a fact for a test and immediately forget the material the moment the test is over. You skim an interesting news article on your phone, but an hour later your brain has failed to retain a single detail. Your teenager explains how to do something on your computer, but when you try to do it again on your own, the instructions no longer make sense.

Other knowledge is useful countless times. When you understand *why* something happened or *how* something works, you can apply that knowledge again and again. For example:

A student who learns the fundamental principles of any discipline can then easily apply that understanding in a variety of ways over time.

An entrepreneur who learns what their customers really want can apply that knowledge to any number of different products and services.

A manager who learns how to unify their team can apply that approach with many future teams.

A person who understands how to make a decision can make decisions forever.

Learning the right thing once is a bargain. A one-time investment of energy up front yields Effortless Results again and again over time.

Find Commonalities

Peter Kaufman, editor of *Poor Charlie's Almanack,* wanted to understand "how everything in the world works." Normally, such a lofty goal would be overwhelming, even laughable. Most of us would give up such a quest before it had even begun. So he found a shortcut. Over a six-month period, he read the condensed interview at the end of every copy of *Discover* magazine ever published online:

144 interviews in all. Each was a short but high-quality summary of some aspect of science, written for a lay audience, with clear examples, engaging stories, and concise language.

He soon found he could separate everything he was learning into three buckets of data. Bucket 1 was the oldest and largest data set: the inorganic universe. It was physics and geology, covering the more than thirteen billion years since the dawn of the universe. Bucket 2 was biology, everything alive on planet Earth. That covered about three billion years. Bucket 3 was the whole of human history: the relatively short period we have been around as a species.

Then he looked for commonalities: principles that could explain how things worked consistently, across all three buckets.

In bucket 1 he found Newton's Third Law of Motion: for every action, there is an equal and opposite reaction. In other words, the more force you exert on something, the more force that thing exerts back. In bucket 2 he found Mark Twain's example of what happens if you pick up a cat by its tail: it will attack you. In bucket 3 he found something similar: how we treat other people is how they will treat us back.

The commonality was a principle that he dubbed "mirrored reciprocation," or, in simpler terms, "You get what you give." Just think of all the ways we can apply that principle! Send a thank-you note, and you will get one back. Smile sincerely at someone, and they will smile back at you. Offer information to someone in a conversation, and they will tend to share information with you in return.

In one experiment investigating the principle of mirrored reciprocation, a researcher sent handwritten Christmas cards to almost six hundred complete strangers. Each card included a note and a photograph of his family. It didn't take long before these complete strangers started sending responses. In all he received close to two hundred cards in reply.

Universal principles don't just apply to science. In fact, they can provide similarly useful mental shortcuts for understanding people.

When I was first married, I once decided to surprise my wife by picking up a meat feast pizza, which I knew she liked. When she came home late that night she was, as I had hoped, delighted.

So the next night I enthusiastically repeated the exercise, surprising her, once again, with a meat feast pizza.

She was so polite that it wasn't until I "surprised" her for the third night in a row that she said, "Oh, meat feast pizza *again*?"

Clearly, the method I had employed so successfully on the first night could be applied only so many times: once in this case!

What if, instead of repeating this method (a few too many times), I'd sought out a *principle* that captured who my wife really was: what she really valued, what consistently delighted her (for more than three evenings in a row). It takes more investment up front to gain this depth of insight. However, once you have it, you can apply it again and again.

Grow a Knowledge Tree

Many people assume that Elon Musk, the founder of Tesla and SpaceX, has a background in mechanical engineering and rocket science. But he actually didn't know much about either subject when he started these ventures.

He was once asked how he had downloaded whole, complex new disciplines into his brain so quickly: "I know you've read a lot of books and you hire a lot of smart people and soak up what they know, but you have to acknowledge you seem to have found a way to pack more knowledge into your head than nearly anyone else alive. How are you so good at it?"

He replied: "It is important to view knowledge as sort of a semantic tree—make sure you understand the fundamental principles, i.e. the trunk and big branches, before you get into the leaves/ details or there is nothing for them to hang on to."

In other words, when we have the solid fundamentals of knowledge, we have somewhere to hang the additional information we learn. We can anchor it in the mental models we already understand.

Musk's approach is supported by the science of how we learn. Neuroplasticity is our brain's ability to change, both at the individual neuron level and at the very complex level of learning a new skill, like learning how to make a rocket. Learning something new is often a series of attempts, failures, and adjustments. Neural connections that result in success are reinforced and grow stronger. Like a tree that can support the growth of new branches as it grows thicker and stronger, our brains can now grow connections, incorporating that new information into our existing foundation of knowledge. Meanwhile, unproductive connections eventually become weaker and, like dead branches, break off.

This is how Musk's search for the fundamentals, the first principles, has allowed him to revolutionize the energy industry, launch broadband satellites into space, design a system for high-speed hyperloop travel, build a better solar battery, and send a spacecraft to Mars. He is living proof that by understanding things at their most fundamental level, we can apply them in new and surprising ways.

Learn the Best of What Others Have Already Figured Out

As vice-chairman of Berkshire Hathaway, ninety-six-year-old Charlie Munger is Warren Buffett's right-hand man. But he's also an investing legend in his own right. In the 1960s and '70s, Munger ran a firm that achieved returns of over 24 percent per year. If you invested $100 in Berkshire stock the day Munger came on board, you'd have over $1.8 million today.

Most professional investors become experts in financial markets. They study the economic forces that drive booms and busts. They learn all there is to know about bond yields, macroeconomics, and small-cap stocks. But Charlie Munger takes a different approach to learning.

Isaiah Berlin's original 1953 essay *The Hedgehog and the Fox* revived the saying by the ancient Greek poet Archilochus, "The fox knows many things, but the hedgehog knows one big thing." Jim Collins famously favored the hedgehog's approach to succeeding in the business world, arguing that foxes lack focus and waste their energy. But Archilochus's comparison was always meant to suggest that the fox would fare better if it didn't simply know many things but knew how to connect those things together. Munger is a fox who connects many things.

Munger's approach to investing and life is the pursuit of what he calls "worldly wisdom." He believes that by combining learnings from a range of disciplines—psychology, history, mathematics, physics, philosophy, biology, and more—we produce something that is greater than the sum of its parts. Munger sees isolated facts as useless unless they "hang together on a latticework of theory."

Different ideas in isolation represent linear knowledge. But those same ideas form residual knowledge when interconnected. Munger acolyte Tren Griffin gives the following example: A business raises the price of its product, yet sells more of that product. This does not make sense if you consider only the discipline of economics and its rule of supply and demand. But if you also consider the discipline of psychology, you understand that buyers think that a higher price means higher quality and therefore buy more.

Often, the most useful knowledge comes from fields other than our own. As researchers from Northwestern University's Kellogg School of Management found in analyzing almost eighteen million scientific papers, the best new ideas usually come from combining existing knowledge in one field with an "intrusion of unusual combinations" from other disciplines. This is why Munger is wise to "believe in the discipline of mastering the best that other people have ever figured out." As he puts it, "I don't believe in just sitting down and trying to dream it all up yourself. Nobody's that smart."

The exchange of ideas across disciplines breeds novelty. And turning the conventional into something novel is often the key to effortless creativity—not only in science but in areas ranging from investing, to music, to making movies.

Before they became household names, best known for Hollywood hits like *Fargo,* directors Joel and Ethan Coen's first blockbuster film was their 1984 neo-noir crime movie *Blood Simple.* When the brothers first read the screenplay though, they were concerned that it followed the pattern of a conventional whodunit. So they took out a pair of scissors and cut out each paragraph from each page of the script. They placed each scrap of paper in a brown paper bag, shook the bag, and tossed the scraps in the air. Then they picked the scraps up off the floor, put them back together randomly, and rewrote the script on that basis. *Blood Simple* became known for its conventional neo-noir crime feel heightened by unpredictable twists and turns that were unusual for the genre. Northwestern professor Brian Uzzi describes this approach as taking "extreme novelty" and embedding it in "deep conventionality."

How to Get the Most Out of Reading

Reading a book is among the most high-leverage activities on earth. For an investment more or less equivalent to the length of a single workday (and a few dollars), you can gain access to what the smartest people have already figured out. Reading, that is, reading to really understand, delivers residual results by any estimate.

Unfortunately, very few people take advantage of this. The typical American reads (or partially reads) only four books a year. More than a quarter of Americans don't read books at all. And this trend is worsening.

Reading a book is among the most high-leverage activities on earth.

To get the most out of your reading I recommend the following principles:

Use the Lindy Effect. This law states that the life expectancy of a book is proportional to its current age—meaning, the older a book is, the higher the likelihood that it will survive into the future. So prioritize reading books that have lasted a long time. In other words, read the classics and the ancients.

Read to Absorb (Rather Than to Check a Box). There are books I have technically read but I can't tell you anything about them. On the other hand, there are books I may not have read cover to cover, but I have returned to certain chapters or passages so often that they have become a part of me. Reading a book to earn the right of displaying it on your shelf misses the real point of the exercise. But absorbing yourself fully in a book changes who you are, just as if you had lived the experience yourself.

Distill to Understand. When I finish reading a book, I like to take ten minutes to summarize what I learned from it on a single page in my own words. If you summarize the key learnings from a book you just read, you absorb it more deeply. The process of summarizing, of distilling ideas to their essential essence, helps us turn information into understanding, and understanding into unique knowledge.

Know What No One Else Knows

In the run-up to the 1968 Summer Olympics in Mexico, most people assumed that high jumper Dick Fosbury would place dead last. He was, after all, a gangly twenty-one-year-old civil engineering student with mismatched running shoes and questionable athletic ability. The media called him the "two-legged camel" and described his jumps as "airborne seizures." He was dismissed as a curiosity.

Ever since his sophomore year in high school, Fosbury had struggled to learn the dominant high-jump technique of the time. Incredibly, this technique hadn't changed since the first recorded high-jump event in Scotland in the nineteenth century: jumpers approached the bar either from the side or face on and took off from their inner foot. Slight variations on these techniques had resulted in equally slight improvements to the world record, which had inched up slowly and in tiny increments over the years.

Using the standard approach, a younger Fosbury had failed to jump even the five feet needed to qualify for his high school track meets. Someone bet him that he couldn't jump over a stuffed leather chair. He lost the bet and broke his hand in the crash landing. His coaches urged him to try harder. But the more he practiced this method without seeing any results, the more frustrated he grew.

Finally, Fosbury decided to try a different approach. He knew that the rules required only that competitors jump off one foot at takeoff; they said nothing about how you got over the bar. So he began to apply his growing knowledge of engineering to experiment with other ways of doing the high jump. One such experiment involved approaching the bar backward, headfirst, curving his body over the bar and kicking his legs up in the air at the end—like a parabola.

Critics were not impressed. One newspaper captioned Fosbury's photograph, "World's Laziest High Jumper." Another headline declared, "Fosbury Flops over Bar."

All the while, Fosbury sharpened his technique. His new J-shaped approach gave him more speed. He began rotating his hips in his final steps and taking off from his outer, rather than inner, foot so that, as his body arched over the bar, he faced up and his center of gravity was underneath. Fosbury had used all that he knew about physical science to create a mechanical advantage. And it worked.

In the world of high jumping there is before October 20, 1968, and there is after. Fosbury won gold that day at the Mexico Olympics, stunning the crowd with what had now been (nonderisively) dubbed the Fosbury Flop. Before him, no Olympic jumper had faced skyward. After him, all world record holders did.

The power of Fosbury's technique lay not only in its solid mechanical foundation but in its uniqueness. It was so different from what others had been doing for decades that it caused a hockey-stick-shaped spike in high-jump world records. Who knows how long such progress would otherwise have taken with only incremental advances in technique? Fosbury achieved the dream harbored by every serious athlete: he transformed his sport forever.

Being good at what nobody is doing is better than being great at what everyone is doing. But being an expert in something nobody is doing is exponentially more valuable.

To reap the residual results of knowledge, the first step is to leverage what others know. But the ultimate goal is to identify knowledge that is unique to you, and build on it. Is there something that seems hard for other people but easy for you? Something that draws on what you already know, making it easier to continuously learn and grow your competence? That is an opportunity for you to create unique knowledge.

Knowledge may open the door to *an* opportunity, but unique knowledge produces *perpetual* opportunities.

You gain credibility. People come to you. Opportunities come to you. You gain incredible leverage when you are among the *only* people with that precise expertise.

In other words, once you develop a reputation for knowing what no one else knows, opportunities flow to you for years. For example:

An entrepreneur with a great reputation will have investor capital flow *to them* again and again.
A speaker with a great reputation will be offered more bookings than they can possibly accept.
A teacher with a great reputation will have students lining up to take their class semester after semester.
A lawyer with a great reputation will have their pick of cases.
A photojournalist with a great reputation will be sent on the best assignments, all over the world.

It happened to me with *Essentialism*. I wrote the book once, but readers reach out to me on a daily basis still.

Gaining unique knowledge takes time, dedication, and effort. But invest in it once, and you'll attract opportunities for the rest of your life.

CHAPTER 12

LIFT

Harness the Strength of Ten

When the COVID-19 pandemic was in its early stages in the United States, there was a shortage of clinical face masks for healthcare workers. As the supply of commercially produced masks continued to dwindle, it became clear that a more "DIY" type of solution was urgently needed.

If you needed to make one face mask for yourself or for a loved one, the easiest route would probably be to look up instructions and make it yourself. But what if the demand was for millions of masks within a few weeks?

Enter *Project*Protect, a collaboration among various community groups in Utah. Their goal was to create five million masks in five weeks. Their method was to teach other people how to create the masks—and to make it easy for them to teach others.

The first people were taught directly. Then the method was recorded, and a five-minute video was put up on their website teaching exactly how to do it and calling for volunteers. *Project*Protect would provide the materials, and the volunteers would pick up as many packs as they could sew—or teach other people to sew—and return the finished masks.

Within the first week, ten thousand volunteers had delivered the first million masks. Within five weeks, fifty thousand volunteers reached their seemingly impossible goal of five million masks. Imagine how much time and effort it would have taken one person, or ten people, or even a hundred people to do that. It was an astonishing achievement, especially when you consider that almost none of the volunteers knew how to make these masks at the beginning of that five weeks.

Whenever we want a far-reaching impact, teaching others to teach can be a high-leverage strategy.

Use Stories to Turn Your Audience into Teachers

A few years ago, my grandfather died in New York City. Since I was the only other family member living in the United States, it fell to me to go through his apartment and sift through all his belongings. And when I did, here is what I found: nothing.

There were books and clothes. There were a few paintings and photos. There was an address book. But the narrative about the life that he had lived, about what really mattered to him, had gone with him. I remember looking through the names in his address book and having no idea who was a lifelong friend and who a one-time acquaintance. None of the names meant anything to me. But they had meant something to him. Suddenly I was aware, in a way that I never had fully been before, of how much of ourselves we take with us in the end. Unintentionally, we often leave only pathetically small clues for those who come after us.

It amazes me how easy it is to forget previous generations. Most people cannot tell you the first and last names of their eight great-grandparents. Ponder that for a moment. The language we speak, the place we live, and the history we inherit are shaped by ancestors we don't even know the names of. A lot is lost in those decayed memories—so much that many of us, once we reach a certain age, find ourselves struck by a curiosity so powerful that we are compelled to track down any available clues about our ancestry.

It turns out there is a far simpler way to pass our history on to future generations: through the sharing of family stories. Stories are bridges from past to present. They make history come alive. They expand our sense of self.

I know of one family who get together once a year for the sole purpose of keeping previous generations alive. They bring photo albums. They create slide decks filled with memories. They share their favorite stories of specific ancestors. They have been doing this now for fifty years.

There is no better way to teach than through the power of stories. Indeed, the right story can live on for millennia. Just think of Aesop's Fables.

Aesop was a storyteller and a slave. He lived more than 2,500 years ago in ancient Greece. He had lessons he wanted to impart, and he did so through memorable stories. His stories were so easy to remember and share, they were passed down by word of mouth.

We love stories. We understand stories. We remember stories. And that means it's easier to share, or to teach, stories. Stories have the power to turn any audience into a roomful of teachers.

When You Learn to Teach, You Teach Yourself to Learn

Teaching others is also an accelerated way to learn. Even thinking we *might* be called upon to teach can increase our engagement. We focus more intently. We listen to understand. We think about the underlying logic so we can put the ideas into our own words.

Since writing *Essentialism*, I have been blessed with many opportunities to teach its principles and practices. And in teaching the ideas, I continue to learn. Indeed, every time I teach an audience about how to be an Essentialist, I learn something new about how to be a better Essentialist in my own life. For example, in learning how one Essentialist applied the ideas, I was inspired to start a new practice. Every day I leave my home office, I call out the time I leave. I am like a town crier. "It's 5:01 P.M.!" I do it loud. I do it for fun. But I also do it for my own accountability: to live what I am teaching.

Think about how hard it is to recall the route we've taken dozens of times until we have to give someone else directions—or how hard it is to fully absorb the plot of a novel you read until you've described it to someone.

Follow the Sesame Street Rule

The head of marketing at a major, international software business I worked with was frustrated. He had expended a lot of personal effort to get the whole company on the same page. He had paid internal and external management consultants to craft a strategy. He had given presentations on the strategy to people within the company. He was consistent in the way he shared this strategy with customers. And yet, it was a mess. Some salespeople explained it one way. Others explained it a different way. Employees all had their own varying interpretations. It was like they were speaking a different language. For a company of a hundred thousand employees in 130 countries, getting people simply to understand the strategy—never mind implement it—was proving a heroic challenge.

Then a different idea was floated: to simplify the message to a short whiteboard sketch that could be explained in under ten minutes. The head of marketing taught it to a pilot group first. Then he had them practice coming to the front of the room and teaching it to one another. Then he sent them off to go and teach it to their teams. Everyone was expected not only to learn it but also to learn how to teach it. Anyone could be asked to stand up in front of any group and teach it at any time. Within just a few weeks, the inconsistencies disappeared. An HR rep in Germany could explain it. A finance manager in California could explain it in the exact same way. This meant that customers were getting the same message as well. Pretty soon, the impact began to multiply. What had once involved months of frustrating effort became a virtually effortless path to success.

If you try to teach people everything about everything, you run the risk of teaching them nothing. You will achieve residual results faster if you clearly identify—then simplify—the most important messages you want to teach others to teach.

These messages should be not just easy to understand but also hard to *mis*understand. A. G. Lafley, the former CEO of Procter & Gamble, called this the "Sesame Street Simple" rule. Don't go for the overly sophisticated message. Don't go for the one that makes you sound smart. Go for the straightforward message that can be easily understood and repeated.

Make the most essential things the easiest ones to teach and the easiest ones to learn.

Chapter 13

AUTOMATE

Do It Once and Never Again

When our children were toddlers, we lived next door to a family quite similar to our own. They had two young children, just like us. We traveled in the same social circles and saw each other every weekend. Even the floor plan of their house was literally the mirror image of ours.

One day the husband told me about his recent knee surgery. All had appeared to go well during the procedure, but his recovery was not progressing as expected. Instead of subsiding, the pain had increased as the weeks went by. Eventually they got to the bottom of the matter: the surgical team had inadvertently left a small surgical instrument inside his knee.

One would never expect this kind of mistake from highly trained medical professionals. And the team that performed the surgery was indeed highly trained. They had degrees from top medical schools. They had many years of experience. Still, in the midst of this complex operation, they made a shockingly careless, utterly avoidable mistake.

The explanation for this is simple: they had relied on their memory. As a result, they forgot an essential step in the process. It's tempting to say, "If only the medical staff had been *thinking*. . . ." But I see it as "If only the medical staff *had not needed to think*. . . ."

Alfred North Whitehead, the British mathematician turned American philosopher, once said, "Civilization advances by extending the number of important operations we can perform without thinking about them"—another way of saying, "As many essential steps and activities as possible should be automated."

Is There a Cheat Sheet for This?

In 1935, rival aircraft companies Boeing, Martin, and Douglas were competing for a lucrative contract to build new long-range bombers. Boeing was expected to win. Its more powerful Model 299 had four engines instead of two. It could carry five times the specified number of bombs and had a range twice as long as its predecessors.

That all changed after its fateful test run. Carrying five crew members, the Model 299 rose gracefully off the runway before stalling at three hundred feet, tipping sharply, and crashing to the ground. Two of the crew were killed, including test pilot Major Ployer P. Hill.

An investigation found that Major Hill, an Army Air Corps pilot with over seventeen years of experience, had forgotten to release the rudder and elevator controls: a fatal error. More instructive, however, was the finding that Hill had been preoccupied by a myriad of other new complex procedures at the exact time he should have been executing these essential tasks. The army concluded that the Model 299—the most technologically sophisticated aircraft of its time—was too complicated for one person to fly and awarded the contract to Douglas.

But a group of test pilots still believed that the Boeing plane was superior and would give the country a distinct military advantage. They simply needed a tool that would allow a single pilot to manage the advanced aeronautical technology.

As the surgeon and bestselling author Dr. Atul Gawande explains in his book *The Checklist Manifesto,* Major Hill's tragic oversight resulted from the very same human limitation that leads to avoidable surgical errors.

The vast amount of knowledge humankind has now acquired in so many disciplines has fueled extraordinary scientific, technological, and humanistic progress. But as Gawande argues, this progress has a downside. The staggering volume and complexity of know-how has exceeded experts' ability to manage it. And this is exactly why tragic accidents happen.

Humans have a tremendous capacity for the storage of memories. Paul Reber, professor of psychology at Northwestern University, estimates that if the brain were a digital video recorder (DVR) it would have enough memory to hold three million hours of TV shows. But the RAM for information we can call up on demand, essentially our working memory, is far more limited. This at least partially explains why highly intelligent people may still forget their keys, or why doctors with deep expertise still forget to remove an instrument from inside the knee of a patient. The limits of working memory breed avoidable errors.

Extreme complexity only increases the cognitive load, making us that much more prone to errors. So what we need is not more knowledge but new skills and strategies that allow us to apply that knowledge without taxing our working memory. Or as Gawande put it, we need a strategy "that builds on experience and takes advantage of the knowledge people have but somehow also makes up for our inevitable human tendencies. And there is such a strategy—though it will seem almost ridiculous in its simplicity, maybe even crazy to those of us who have spent years carefully developing ever more advanced skills and technologies."

What we need, Gawande argues, is a modest but marvelous tool: the checklist.

Once the Boeing test pilots implemented checklists and flew over and over without incident, Gawande writes, the Army Air Corps ordered thousands of the planes. Renamed the B-17, the Model 299 dropped more bombs than any other US aircraft in World War II and helped turn the tide for the Allies.

The checklist helped the pilots remember each and every essential step, using as few mental resources as possible.

The checklist isn't just useful for highly specialized tasks like flying an airplane. As the world gets more complex, we all need tools to help us remember what's important.

The beauty of the checklist is that the thinking has been done ahead of time. It's been taken out of the equation. Or rather, it has been baked into the equation. So instead of getting these essential things right occasionally, we get them right every time.

A cheat sheet is one of the most effective, albeit low-tech, tools we have at our disposal to automate almost anything that really matters. The checklist is one type. Here are a few others:

An employee uses daily planning software to make it easy to prioritize their day.
A manager creates an agenda for their weekly meeting to ensure they cover the most important topics.
An entrepreneur brings a slide deck to each pitch meeting to make it easy to remember the most salient points to cover.
A teacher gives his students a list of writing tips to make it easy to write a great essay.

A parent creates a chore calendar that makes it easier for the kids to remember who is responsible for what each day.

Of course, this is just a partial list. The idea of a cheat sheet is simply to get things out of your brain so you can do them automatically, without having to rely on memory.

Residual Results for One Hundred Years

Have you ever been frustrated by the process of deciding where to go for an extended family holiday? Too many opinions. Too many schedules. Too many options. It can add up to months of going back and forth. And once you figure it out, you have the whole process to look forward to next year.

Stephen and Irene Richards had a different idea. They wanted to make it easy for their children to get together regularly. So they decided to automate the process of choosing a destination and planning a new trip every year. They invested in a small lodge in Montana. Every summer, everyone was invited to go for as much or as little time as they wanted.

This grew into a ritual people looked forward to. It became self-perpetuating. Every year, their children came. Eventually their children got married and had children of their own, and those children started coming too. Their children, grandchildren, and great-grandchildren eventually built new lodges in the area. And so it has continued to expand.

Now, a full five generations later, the family still gets together to play, swim, and make memories each and every year. On any given summer day, thirty to forty family members will be out playing on the beach by the lake. On some days the party swells to more than one hundred people.

Making decisions is mentally draining. Making decisions that will satisfy dozens of other people, each with different preferences, constraints, and priorities, is both mentally draining and close to impossible. That single decision made so many years ago eliminated this burden for seven generations of Richardses—and counting. Nobody has to do the work of coordinating everyone's schedules and choosing a destination, booking hotels, and planning activities in order for the whole family to spend time together. It is automatic and, compared to some family vacation planning I have seen, effortless.

High Tech = Low Effort

"Admittedly I was a bit careless when I started driving," a then-eighteen-year-old Joshua Browder sheepishly says when asked about the ten traffic tickets he racked up in his first year of driving. But in Browder's view, most of his infractions either didn't merit a ticket or were the result of errors by the infamous traffic wardens, the UK's parking enforcement officers.

So Browder decided to appeal the tickets. It turned out the courts agreed with him and he began winning his appeals. It didn't take long before he was helping almost everyone he knew to contest unfair tickets. The appeal process was relatively formulaic; a simple boilerplate letter was often enough to avoid an unwarranted fine. But while navigating the bureaucracy may have been simple for him, he noticed that for the elderly, disabled, and otherwise vulnerable people in his community, it was anything but. This gave him an idea for how he could do some good. It took Browder, who was then still a student at Stanford, just two weeks to build DoNotPay, a website (and later, an app) dubbed "the World's First Robot Lawyer" that automated the process of appeals for those in need.

Building on the success of the concept, Browder soon added a service that automatically scans users' email inbox for travel reservations, then helps them capitalize on price drops on flight and hotel reservations. Anyone can simply click the "Solve This Problem for Me" button and the automated process will take over.

The app now saves users time and money by scheduling appointments with the DMV, getting them refunds from GrubHub, and unsubscribing them from spam—and even automatically adding them as a plaintiff to any existing legal claims against the spammer.

Automation is anything that performs a function with minimal human assistance or effort. And it's happening everywhere. Some of it is so normal we don't really think of it as automation: the washing machine, dishwasher, refrigerator. It's only when these things malfunction or break that we stop to think about how much time and effort they save us on a daily basis.

Other forms of automation haven't been around as long but are still familiar enough that we don't notice them anymore: automatic bill pay, the programmable thermostat, your virtual assistant reminding you what's on your shopping list, and so on.

These tools are getting smarter all the time. Your virtual assistant can use AI algorithms to analyze your past buying patterns to tell you when you might be running out of shampoo or toothpaste. Your thermostat can learn how warm or cool you like to keep your home throughout the day and adjust itself accordingly.

Already, so many mental tasks can be offloaded onto technology—and this trend is only accelerating. After all, the technology for self-driving cars is effectively here now.

In 2012, leaders at Expedia discovered that for every one hundred people who booked a reservation on their site, fifty-eight people needed additional assistance and called their customer service line. The number one reason customers called was that they needed their itinerary re-sent to them. That added up to twenty million calls a year: approximately the equivalent of every person in Australia calling the company every year. The CEO at the time said that if each call cost $5, which he felt was a low estimate, then this added up to at least a $100 million problem.

So instead of continuing to respond to each of these requests one by one, Expedia made it possible for customers to access their itinerary right on the website and through an automated message system. It required a modest investment of time and effort up front, but the result of that one action was a 43 percent reduction in calls each day from then on.

The time and cost savings from this single change were so significant that today the company is rolling out a whole host of self-service features that use artificial intelligence and machine learning to meet customers' varied and ever-evolving needs. Ryan O'Neill, who heads Expedia's customer experience operations, expects that eventually 90 to 95 percent of all customer service functions will be fully automated.

How can we use technology to automate the things that really matter in our own everyday lives?

Essential Domains	Effortless Automation
Your health	Schedule your annual physical as a recurring appointment on the same day each year, and your dentist appointments on the same day every six months. Sign up for regular delivery and automated payment of your recurring medicines from your pharmacy. Set your phone to turn on "nightlight" mode two hours before bedtime.
Your relationships	Set up regular calls or get-togethers with the people who matter most. Set calendar reminders for friend and family member birthdays. Preorder flowers or gifts to be sent on key birthdays, anniversaries, or other annual events.

Your finances	Have a percentage of your paycheck automatically deposited in savings each month. Schedule a weekly meeting to review your finances as a family, and annual meetings with a financial adviser. Automate budgeting with an app that tracks your spending. Set up regular monthly or annual donations to your most valued charities.
Your home	Subscribe for regular online purchases of key items for the home. Create an annual safety checklist for things like smoke detectors and fire extinguishers. Set up recurring shopping lists in a grocery store app. Delegate meal planning to an app based on your health goals.
Your career	Schedule recurring meetings with a mentor. Schedule an hour every quarter to review your personal career goals. Block off five minutes every morning to read an article on an important topic not directly related to your job.
Your fun	Block off one hour each day for something that brings you joy.

Blocking off time for the things that matter may sound simple in theory. But in practice it can be difficult to do consistently, because reality gets in the way. Yet the effort we invest in automating our most mundane but essential tasks yields significant and repeated benefits later on.

One caveat is important to make at this juncture: automation can work for you or against you. If nonessential activities are automated, they too continue to happen without you thinking about it.

Take, for example, subscriptions that renew automatically. We always think we'll remember to discontinue them, but we never do, and we end up being charged for months or even years without knowing it. I once realized I was paying ten times the correct amount to an online service I had signed up for; instead of the $10 a month I thought I was being charged, I had in fact been charged $100 for several months before I noticed. Consider taking the high-tech, low-effort path for the essential, and the low-tech, high-effort path for the nonessential.

CHAPTER 14

TRUST

The Engine of High-Leverage Teams

In 2003, Warren Buffett, one of the most successful investors in the world and the chairman and CEO of Berkshire Hathaway, was interested in buying McLane Distribution, a $23 billion provider of supply chain solutions that was owned by Wal-Mart. We'd be safe to assume that making that happen would be a huge and extraordinarily complex undertaking.

Just the due diligence, or the process of confirming that what he had been told about the business was accurate, would take monumental effort. It would require dozens of attorneys reading every contract, equipment lease, real estate purchase document, and union agreement. It would take a small army of accountants going over every line item on the company's annual, quarterly, and monthly financial statements, combing through every asset, lien, and debt. It would take a team of compliance officers to audit, investigate, and verify every capital expenditure, legacy technology, and stated risk. It would likely involve looking into relationships with

McLane's top customers. All of this could easily have added up to millions of dollars and taken six months or more to complete.

Which makes what actually happened so incredible: Buffett closed the McLane deal over a single two-hour meeting and a handshake. Just twenty-nine days later the purchase was complete. Buffett wrote, "We did no 'due diligence.'" On the basis of his prior experience, he concluded he "knew everything would be exactly as Wal-Mart said it would be—and it was."

A two-hour meeting and a handshake? With no due diligence! Think of the time, money, and effort saved, based on the simple fact that one party trusted the other to be true to their word. It's an example of how trust can be a lever for turning modest effort into residual results.

All of us work with other human beings in some capacity. Some of us do it in highly matrixed organizations where we report to more than one person, deal with internal and external customers, and have to coordinate across siloed departments and/or functional groups. Some of us work in and across smaller teams that are expected to function nimbly, get things done quickly, and produce more with fewer resources. Even those of us who work for ourselves have to manage relationships with clients and customers, coordinate deliverables with suppliers and partners, and so on. Each of these environments adds layers of complexity: some avoidable, others not.

We all work with other people in our personal lives too. And here also people are a source of complexity. There are coordinating schedules in and across our immediate family, extended family, blended families. There is managing relationships within our friend groups, and negotiating competing desires within our local community.

No matter the context, working with other people can be overwhelming. You have to allocate mental resources. You have to preserve relationships. You have to align diverse or competing priorities. Just think of the effort involved in deciding where to eat when you're getting together with a big group of friends or family. The more people involved, the higher the coordination costs. Even easy decisions can become much harder than they need to be.

There is an easier way to get the right things done together.

When you have trust in your relationships, they take less effort to maintain and manage. You can quickly split work between team members. People can talk about problems when they come up, openly and honestly. Members share valuable information rather than hoard it. Nobody minds asking questions when they don't understand something. The speed and quality of decisions go up. Political infighting goes down. You may even enjoy the experience of working together. And you perform exponentially better, because you're able to focus all your energy and attention on getting important things done, rather than on simply getting along.

When you have low trust on teams, everything is hard. Just sending a text or an email is exhausting as you weigh up every word for how it might be taken. When the response comes back you may experience a jolt of anxiety. Every conversation feels like it's a grind. When you don't trust that someone will deliver, you will feel you need to check up on them: remind them of deadlines, hover over them, review their work. Or you won't delegate anything at all, assuming you're better off just doing it yourself. The work can start to stall altogether.

You can't have a high-performing team without high levels of trust.

Trust Is the Engine Oil for High-Performing Teams

We all know that you need to add oil to a car engine in order to keep it operating. But not everyone understands exactly why. It's because inside the engine, the many fast-moving parts can create friction when they rub up against each other. The oil is the lubricant that keeps those parts sliding smoothly, instead of wearing each other down. This is why, if the engine runs out of oil, your car will stall or even grind to a halt.

Sounds a lot like what happens on low-trust teams, doesn't it? Inside every team are many people with interrelated roles and responsibilities, moving at high speeds. Without trust, conflicting goals, priorities, and agendas rub up against each other, creating friction and wearing everyone down. If the team runs out of trust, it is likely to stall or sputter out. Trust is like the engine oil for that team. It's the lubricant that keeps these people working together smoothly, so the team can continue to function.

The key to getting Effortless Results in and across teams is to have systems in place to ensure that the engine is constantly well oiled.

The Hire That's Worth More Than a Hundred Other Hires

The best way to leverage trust to get residual results is simply to select trustworthy people to be around.

Steve Hall, a successful entrepreneur, told me about a controller he once hired to help manage the finances for his automotive company. It wasn't until the controller had been with the company for five years that Steve stumbled on a $300,000 accounting discrepancy. When he questioned the controller, she was apologetic: she made it seem like a well-intentioned mistake. But Steve and his CFO had their doubts. They were no longer sure they could trust her in that position and decided to find a replacement. However, this all came at a time when the business was growing rapidly, and they didn't want to deal with the potential disruption. So instead of firing her, they decided to build support around her.

Five years later they discovered that the $300,000 "mistake" had turned into $1.6 million stolen from the business. When she learned that she'd been caught, she resigned via text message and left town. No one at the company ever heard from her again.

In hindsight, Steve admits, "My mistake was even worse than hiring someone I didn't trust. I hired her, she lost my trust, and I continued to have her stay on long after she lost my trust."

Hiring someone trustworthy starts a simple and obvious first step, but one that many routinely overlook: making sure you are hiring someone honest and honorable, someone you can trust to uphold a high standard when nobody's looking. But hiring someone who is trustworthy is also about hiring someone conscientious, someone you can trust to uphold their responsibilities, to use good judgment, to do what they say they're going to do when they say they're going to do it and to do it well. It's someone you don't have to supervise or micromanage, someone who understands the team's goals and who cares as much as you do about the quality of the essential work to be done.

Warren Buffett uses three criteria for determining who is trustworthy enough to hire or to do business with. He looks for people with integrity, intelligence, and initiative, though he adds that without the first, the other two can backfire.

I call this "The Three I's Rule."

After the disaster with his controller, Steve Hall had to find a replacement. Rather than blaming the whole thing on "just one bad apple," he and the CFO looked long and hard for any ways in which they might have unwittingly enabled the problem to occur. This honest self-assessment helped them see how they needed to improve their hiring process. They had hired the most recent controller haphazardly, by way of an off-the-cuff suggestion from a supplier. Going forward they committed to a new process; it involved more time and effort up front, but Steve now understood that investing wisely in recruiting, interviewing, and onboarding once could reduce his risk many, many times over.

His new hiring criteria mirrored the Three I's Rule.

In the end they hired a man who had no experience in the automotive industry; he'd run accounting for a law firm. But he was a complete fit on integrity, intelligence, and initiative: a self-starter with an unimpeachable ethic and the ability to figure out problems on the fly. Or, put more simply, they really trusted him. Austin has been a valued member of the company for years now. Even after the business was sold to a Fortune 500 company, he was kept on. He's been promoted three times since. The high-trust hire turned out to be one of the company's highest performers.

When you can say these four little words, "I trust your judgment"—and mean them—it's like magic. Team members feel empowered. They take a risk. They grow. Trust is strengthened. And then it tends to spread. As executive coach Kim Scott writes in her bestselling book *Radical Candor,* "When people trust you and believe you care about them, they are more likely to . . . engage in this same behavior with one another, meaning less pushing the rock up the hill again and again."

Hiring someone is a single decision that produces Effortless Results. You get it right once, and that person adds value hundreds of times over. You get it wrong once, and it can cost you repeatedly. It's like skimping on a shoddy oil filter. It might keep the engine running smoothly in the short term, but the moment that filter starts leaking, it will cause problems throughout the system.

Who we hire is a disproportionately important decision that makes a thousand other decisions. Each new hire may well influence future hires, gradually shifting the norms and the culture over time.

Often, there will be pressure to fill a role immediately, as the vacancy creates a short-term headache. But while hiring quickly may lighten the load at first, hiring *well* will lighten the load consistently and repeatedly, saving you many more headaches in the long run.

Create a High-Trust Agreement

There are three parties to every relationship: Person A, Person B, and the structure that governs them.

When trust becomes an issue, most people point at the other person. The manager blames the employee; the employee blames the manager. The teacher blames the student; the student blames the teacher. The parent blames the child; the child blames the parent. Sometimes we are able to recognize that *we* were the ones at fault. But we rarely think to blame the structure of the relationship itself.

Every relationship has a structure, even if it's an unspoken, unclear one. A low-trust structure is one where expectations are unclear, where goals are incompatible or at odds, where people don't know who is doing what, where the rules are ambiguous and nobody knows what the standards for success are, and where the priorities are unclear and the incentives misaligned.

A high-trust structure is one where expectations are clear. Goals are shared, roles are clearly delineated, the rules and standards are articulated, and the right results are prioritized, incentivized, and rewarded—consistently, not just sometimes.

Most people can agree that this type of relationship is preferable. The problem is that low-trust relationship structures generally happen by default rather than by design.

I once hired several professionals to help us remodel our home. They were employed by three different companies but had worked together on a variety of projects over many years. They liked one another. They seemed competent. Each individual had come highly recommended. I thought the pieces were in place for a high-trust experience.

I began to worry only after I asked for a written agreement with dates attached to it and never received one. But I was eager for the renovations to get going and decided it wasn't worth pausing the work until we had it. This turned out to be shortsighted.

While each person on the team worked competently enough on their own, as a team they were far from cohesive. There was no parallel processing. There were no clear work flows. A vendor would complete a task, and only then would the next piece of work be ordered. So some of the cabinets would get installed, while others would be delayed for weeks.

There was miscommunication: sometimes workers would turn up to work but the materials hadn't arrived. They couldn't agree on deadlines. They couldn't agree on who was responsible for what, so some efforts got duplicated while others slipped through the cracks. We were given incorrect dimensions for an appliance, so it needed to be reordered from a different manufacturer altogether to fit in the limited space.

The end result? The remodel was completed late and over budget. And the experience for everyone involved was harder at every turn than it needed to be. That's the typical outcome when you have a low-trust structure.

A couple of years after this frustrating experience I was invited to speak to the Lean Construction Institute (LCI), a trade association working to address the decline in efficiency within the construction industry. While other labor-intensive industries have seen efficiency improve since the 1960s, today in the United States a whopping 70 percent of construction projects are delivered late and over budget, and, more concerningly, eight hundred construction-related deaths and thousands more injuries are reported each year.

The LCI sees lean principles as being key to improving this situation.

One solution is a unique business contract they refer to as "the Deal" that ties each participant's compensation to the outcome of the whole project rather than to the work that individual contributed. Aligning the incentives in this way encourages the different parties to act as one team and to make decisions that benefit the whole project rather than their own self-interest. They not only feel a sense of ownership but are motivated to take initiative to make the whole experience more efficient.

Whether we're remodeling a home or leading a team of colleagues, we can all create a similar high-trust agreement to make it easier to get the right things done together. Even a one-time investment in such an agreement can pay dividends. And it can be as simple as sitting down together and codifying the following:

High-Trust Agreement

Results	What results do we want?
Roles	Who is doing what?
Rules	What minimum viable standards must be kept?
Resources	What resources (people, money, tools) are available and needed?
Rewards	How will progress be evaluated and rewarded?

Taking a little time to build a foundation of trust is a valuable investment in any relationship. It's a lever that turns a modest effort into residual results.

Chapter 15

PREVENT

Solve the Problem Before It Happens

In 1977, Ali Maow Maalin was a hospital cook working in Merca, Somalia. When cases of smallpox broke out, he offered to serve as a guide to local officials who were transporting two afflicted children to an isolation camp. Maalin knew that he should get vaccinated before traveling with the highly contagious children, but the injection looked painful. Besides, he reasoned, the journey lasted just ten minutes. Surely, he wouldn't be in contact with the children for long enough to get infected.

By the time he began to display symptoms, he had come in contact with many members of his family, friends, and neighbors. What followed was an intense two-week effort, led by the World Health Organization's eradication team, to vaccinate 54,777 people in the area to ensure the virus would spread no further—efforts that could have been avoided had Maalin received a single injection.

There is a happy ending to this story. This narrowly avoided public health disaster was really the last chapter in the most successful health intervention in history: a multiyear campaign to eradicate smallpox. On April 17, 1978, the WHO's Nairobi office sent a simple message via telegram: "Search complete. No cases discovered. Ali Maow Maalin is the world's last known smallpox case." As a result of health officials' coordinated efforts to vaccinate large swaths of the world's population, a disease that killed three hundred million people in the twentieth century had now been contained to laboratories.

We might not think of prevention as the most obvious way to achieve residual results. But what else can you call it when a single intervention saves an incalculable number of future lives and solves a centuries-long problem once and for all?

The Long Tail of Time Management

John opened a desk drawer to take out a pen. When the drawer stubbornly refused to shut, he went through his usual dance: opening it as far as it would go, shaking it, closing and opening it again, and moving things around. This went on for a while. Intrigued, his colleague, Dean Acheson (a mentor of productivity guru David Allen), asked what was going on. It turned out that a pencil tray was in the way. How long had it been a problem, Dean wanted to know. "Two years," John replied. "For two years I have been bothered by that every single day." How long would it take to solve it? Two minutes. John solved it right then.

Why do so many of us put up with problems—big and small—for so much longer than we have to?

Because on any given day it usually takes less time to manage a problem than to solve it. In John's case, while thirty seconds of jostling was annoying, it still took less time than dislodging the tray and resolving the problem.

But looking at the equation from a longer-term perspective

changes our calculation. Once we add up the cumulative costs of the time and frustration from today, plus tomorrow, plus hundreds of tomorrows after that, suddenly it makes sense to invest in solving the problem once and for all. Using that time frame, fixing that drawer was an absolute bargain: two minutes' worth of effort to prevent hundreds of future frustrations, an impressive time rebate.

This is what I call *the long tail of time management.* When we invest our time in actions with a long tail, we continue to reap the benefits over a long period.

Sometimes we get so used to the little irritations—like a pencil tray lodged in a desk drawer—it doesn't even occur to us to do anything about them. Even if we are bothered by them and we complain about them, we still don't really *see* them as a problem worth fixing. But what we often fail to recognize is that some tasks that seem "not worth it" in the moment may save us one hundred times the time and aggravation over the long run.

To break this habit, ask yourself:

1. What is a problem that irritates me repeatedly?
2. What is the total cost of managing that over several years?
3. What is the next step I can take immediately, in a few minutes, to move toward solving it?

The goal is to find the most annoying thing that can be solved in the least amount of time.

Once you start asking these questions, you'll start noticing the small actions you can take to make your life easier in the future. For example, I once had a client who was chronically late to meetings. She knew that each time it happened it was hurting her reputation and credibility. And any time she saw an important meeting on her calendar, she experienced acute anxiety; ironically, she was so consumed with worry about being late *again,* she would lose track of

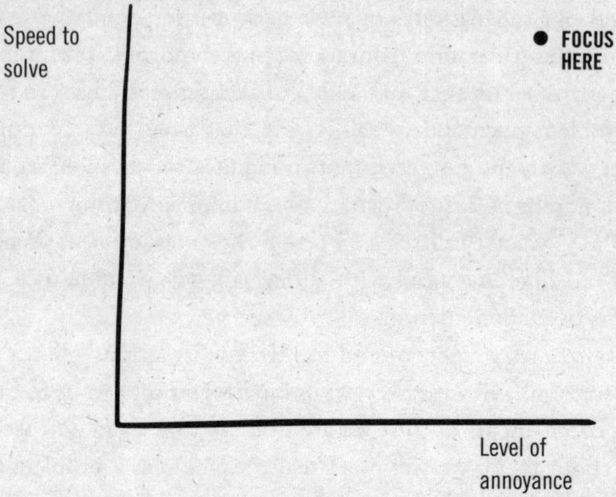

time and her worst fear would be realized. Finally, she found a way to prevent the problem before it happened; each night she spent two minutes reviewing the next day's calendar and setting a reminder to pop up five minutes before each meeting. Simply knowing the reminders were set eased her anxiety, and she soon shed her reputation among colleagues as "the one who is always late."

The Surprising Power of Striking at the Root

Henry David Thoreau once wrote, "There are a thousand hacking at the branches of evil to one who is striking at the root." When we're merely managing a problem, we're hacking at the branches. To prevent the problem before it even arises, we should strike at the root.

If you've spent a lot of time hacking at the branches, you may have become good at it. But if that is all you are doing, the problem will keep coming back to haunt you. It is merely being managed, never solved.

Are there any recurring problems or frustrations in your life or work? Rather than simply hacking at the branches, try striking at the root. For example:

Hack at the Branches	Strike at the Root
A doctor treats a heart problem through years of medication followed by highly invasive surgery.	A doctor encourages patients to eat right, exercise, and schedule regular checkups.
An employee apologizes for completing a project late: repeatedly, to multiple parties.	An employee improves their process so the project is done on time.
An educator constantly complains about students not paying attention in class.	An educator signs a social contract with parents and students regarding expectations before the year begins.
A student is exhausted from always pulling all-nighters before an assignment is due.	A student spends sixty seconds blocking off time to work on assignments every day for a week before they are due.
A parent bemoans having to tidy up after their children every day.	A parent reinforces a positive habit around tidying up.

It's Never Too Early to Sound the Alarm

Suddenly, Mary's heart stopped and her nurse immediately triggered a code blue. She had come to the hospital for routine knee-replacement surgery and was in fairly good health. Now a crash cart team was racing to the operating room to save her life. Thanks to their fast response, Mary became one of the lucky 15 percent of patients who survive a code blue event.

After the dust settled, Mary's nurse was horrified to realize, in retrospect, that she had missed some warning signs. About six hours before the cardiac event, Mary's speech and breathing had become slightly labored, but because her vital signs were normal the nurse wasn't concerned. Two hours later, Mary's oxygen had dipped a little and she told her nurse she was feeling a little tired. The nurse decided not to call a physician because she didn't want to raise a false alarm.

Research shows that patients often display subtle warning signs six to eight hours before a heart attack. But hospital staff members often wait to see more evidence of a serious issue before bringing these small problems to the attention of doctors. Meanwhile, the window of opportunity to prevent a crisis is closing.

Several years ago, Australian hospitals came up with a system to take advantage of that window of opportunity and identify potential cardiac arrests before they happen. They created specialized rapid response teams (RRTs) that included a critical-care nurse, a respiratory therapist, and a physician or a physician's assistant. And in all units they posted a list of the triggers that might signal a cardiac arrest, along with thresholds for action. For example, the nurse must call the RRT if a patient's heart rate falls below 40 beats per minute or rises above 130 beats per minute, even if their vital signs appear normal.

This system was soon adopted by some hospitals in the United States and has resulted in a 71 percent reduction in code blues and an 18 percent reduction in deaths. A physician explained why RRTs proved successful: "The key to this process is time. The sooner you identify a problem, the more likely you are to avert a dangerous situation."

Just as you can find small actions to make your life easier in the future, you can look for small actions that will prevent your life from becoming more complicated. This principle applies in every type of endeavor.

Measure Twice, Cut Once

In 2014, the French satirical newspaper *Le Canard enchaîné* noticed an odd occurrence at railway stations in France. The train platforms seemed to be getting smaller, and nobody seemed to know why. The newspaper contacted SNCF, the country's state-owned railway company, to inquire, but company spokespeople were tight-lipped. So the reporters kept digging.

Finally, the story came out: earlier that year, as part of their efforts to modernize France's rail system, SNCF had spent $20 billion on a new fleet of two thousand trains. The French prided themselves on these modern, state-of-the-art machines. The fact that they were built in France, rather than imported from another country, mattered to them.

There was only one problem: a full quarter of the platforms in France were eight inches too wide for the trains to enter the station. When *Le Canard enchaîné* uncovered the scale of the error and broke the story, SNCF had already quietly shaved eight inches off the edges of three hundred platforms. But one thousand remained. The final cost to French taxpayers? Sixty-five million dollars.

An NPR reporter asked the question on everyone's minds when he interviewed a *Le Canard enchaîné* columnist: "How could the SNCF, a national railroad that's been operating since 1938, do something so dumb as buy trains that don't fit in so many of its stations?"

At first the answer wasn't clear. Then the blamestorming began. The French transport minister called the mistake a "comic drama" and pointed to the previous administration for its decision to split the national train company, SNCF, and the national rail operator, RFF, into two separate state-run entities. Eventually the problem was traced back to a simple and preventable error. RFF, which had given SNCF the dimensions, had measured only platforms built less than thirty years ago, assuming these were representative of all platforms. What they failed to take into account was the fact that many of France's regional platforms had been built more than fifty years ago, when trains were narrower. A spokesman for the RFF unhelpfully commented, "It's as if you have bought a Ferrari that you want to park in your garage, and you realize that your garage isn't exactly the right size to fit a Ferrari because you didn't have a Ferrari before."

Unfortunately, confirmed another spokesperson, they had "discovered the problem a bit late." Indeed.

One small assumption goes unverified. A train gets built and then purchased two thousand times. It's the kind of mistake we've all made, albeit on a significantly smaller scale.

The lesson is one that many of us learned doing arts and crafts as children: measure twice and cut once.

Often, measuring something just once (or not at all) produces *first-order consequences:* the consequences are the direct and immediate results of our actions. In this case, the RFF made a faulty assumption about the uniformity of French station platforms and as a result conveyed inaccurate measurements.

But the chain of consequences, of course, didn't stop there. In an interrelated world, a single action can also have *second-order and third-order consequences.* In this case the inaccurate measurements resulted in the trains being too wide, which resulted in the need for major construction work across three hundred stations, which resulted in a $65 million government expenditure—money that could otherwise have been allocated to schools or hospitals or homeless shelters.

Mistakes are dominoes: they have a cascading effect. When we strike at the root by catching our mistakes *before* they can do any damage, we don't just prevent that first domino from toppling, we prevent the entire chain reaction.

An Effortless Summary

Part I	Effortless State
What is the Effortless State?	The Effortless State is an experience many of us have had when we are physically rested, emotionally unburdened, and mentally energized. You are completely aware, alert, present, attentive, and focused on what's important in this moment. You are able to focus on what matters most with ease.
INVERT	Instead of asking, "Why is this so hard?," invert the question by asking, "What if this could be easy?" Challenge the assumption that the "right" way is, inevitably, the harder one. Make the impossible possible by finding an indirect approach. When faced with work that feels overwhelming, ask, "How am I making this harder than it needs to be?"
ENJOY	Pair the most essential activities with the most enjoyable ones. Accept that work and play can co-exist. Turn tedious tasks into meaningful rituals. Allow laughter and fun to lighten more of your moments.
RELEASE	Let go of emotional burdens you don't need to keep carrying. Remember: When you focus on what you lack, you lose what you have. When you focus on what you have, you get what you lack. Use this habit recipe: "Each time I complain I will say something I am thankful for." Relieve a grudge of its duties by asking, "What job have I hired this grudge to do?"

REST	Discover the art of doing nothing. Do not do more today than you can completely recover from by tomorrow. Break down essential work into three sessions of no more than ninety minutes each. Take an effortless nap.
NOTICE	Achieve a state of heightened awareness by harnessing the power of presence. Train your brain to focus on the important and ignore the irrelevant. To see others more clearly, set aside your opinions, advice, and judgment, and put their truth above your own. Clear the clutter in your physical environment before clearing the clutter in your mind.
Part II	**Effortless Action**
What is Effortless Action?	Effortless Action means accomplishing more by trying less. You stop procrastinating and take the first obvious step. You arrive at the point of completion without overthinking and overthinking. You make progress by pacing yourself rather than powering through. You overachieve without overexerting.
DEFINE	To get started on an essential project, first define what "done" looks like. Establish clear conditions for completion, get there, then stop. Take sixty seconds to focus on your desired outcome. Write a "Done for the Day" list. Limit it to items that would constitute meaningful progress.
START	Make the first action the most obvious one. Break the first obvious action down into the tiniest, concrete step. Then name it. Gain maximum learning from minimal viable effort. Start with a ten-minute microburst of focused activity to boost motivation and energy.

SIMPLIFY	To simplify the process, don't simplify the steps: simply remove them. Recognize that not everything requires you to go the extra mile. Maximize the steps not taken. Measure progress in the tiniest of increments.
PROGRESS	When you start a project, start with rubbish. Adopt a "zero-draft" approach and just put some words, any words, on the page. Fail cheaply: make learning-sized mistakes. Protect your progress from the harsh critic in your head.
PACE	Set an effortless pace: slow is smooth, smooth is fast. Reject the false economy of "powering through." Create the right range: *I will never do less than X, never more than Y.* Recognize that not all progress is created equal.
Part III	**Effortless Results**
What are Effortless Results?	You've continued to cultivate your Effortless State. You've started to take Effortless Action with clarity of objective, tiny, obvious first steps, and a consistent pace. You are achieving the results you want, more easily. But now you want those results to continue to flow to you, again and again, with as little additional effort as possible. You are ready to achieve Effortless Results.
LEARN	Learn principles, not just facts and methods. Understand first principles deeply and then apply them again and again. Stand on the shoulders of giants and leverage the best of what they know. Develop unique knowledge, and it will open the door to perpetual opportunity.

LIFT	Use teaching as a lever to harness the strength of ten. Achieve far-reaching impact by teaching others to teach. Live what you teach, and notice how much you learn. Tell stories that are easily understood and repeated.
AUTOMATE	Free up space in your brain by automating as many essential tasks as possible. Use checklists to get it right every time, without having to rely on memory. Seek single choices that eliminate future decisions. Take the high-tech path for the essential and the low-tech path for the nonessential.
TRUST	Leverage trust as the engine oil of frictionless and high-functioning teams. Make the right hire once, and it will continue to produce results again and again. Follow the Three I's Rule: hire people with integrity, intelligence, and initiative. Design high-trust agreements to clarify results, roles, rules, resources, and rewards.
PREVENT	Don't just manage the problem. Solve it before it happens. Seek simple actions today that can prevent complications tomorrow. Invest two minutes of effort once to end recurring frustrations. Catch mistakes before they happen; measure twice, so you only have to cut once.

Conclusion

NOW

What Happens Next Matters Most

Not long ago my family and I moved into an idyllic community. White picket fences line the streets. There are no streetlamps. There are more horse trails than roads. Our children spent long days playing outside with our happy dog, riding horses, and playing tennis. We took morning walks and bike rides. We planted a garden with apple trees, grapevines, and melon plants. In short, we found ourselves living in a little piece of heaven on earth.

One of our daughters, Eve, seemed especially to thrive. She is a slim, brown-eyed, blond-haired girl with a mischievous grin. She simply cannot stay cross. Even when she *tries* to be grumpy, she can do it for only a few seconds before bursting into laughter. She loves to be in nature. Some family friends of ours still recall how she climbed to the top of their massive fifty-foot fir tree the first time she visited their home. She ran barefoot whenever she could, wrestled with her younger brother on the trampoline for hours at a time, named the chickens, carefully caught lizards by the dozen and gently released them.

Eve read endlessly, devouring books about horses, bees, and insects. Her favorite was a series about a veterinarian's adventures with farm animals and their owners in Yorkshire, England. She wrote about her own adventures in her journal every day. Once, when I took Eve with me on a business trip, I called Anna from the airport and told her Eve literally hadn't stopped talking since we left an hour and a half before. It was animated, scintillating conversation, punctuated with laughter.

Then Eve turned fourteen. She hit a growth spurt, began to feel tired a lot, talked to us less, and took longer to do her chores. So, pretty age-appropriate behavior, or so we thought.

On a routine visit with a physical therapist, he noticed Eve didn't respond properly to basic reflex tests. He took Anna aside and said, "You might want to see a neurologist." We didn't have to be told twice.

From there her symptoms worsened on a daily basis. Within just a few weeks she could answer only in one-word sentences, speaking in a slurred and monotone voice. We noticed that the right-hand side of her body responded at a slower speed than the left-hand side. It took her two full minutes to write her name and hours to eat a meal. The light, once so vibrant and bright in Eve, dimmed. Then it seemed to go out entirely when she was hospitalized after a major seizure.

What made the situation worse was that the doctors couldn't explain any of it. They could not offer us even the beginning of a diagnosis.

Every day brought more visits to respected neurologists who looked at us with furrowed brows; one of them literally shrugged his shoulders. There were tests and tests and more tests. All of them came back negative. The doctors still couldn't find anything, not even a clue. To watch our vivacious daughter in an almost constant state of free fall and have no explanation is the stuff true suffering is made of.

With each unfruitful doctor's visit, each inconclusive test, it became harder and harder to see the road ahead. The challenge before us didn't just feel hard, it felt utterly impossible.

All we wanted in the world was for Eve to get better. That wasn't just the most important thing. It was the only thing.

What came into view for me was two paths for getting there. One made this challenging situation heavier. The other made this challenging situation lighter. And we had to choose which path to take. Maybe this choice seems obvious. But it wasn't.

As parents, our instinct was to attack the problem, with full force, from all directions: worrying about her 24/7, reaching out to every neurologist in the country, meeting with doctors one after the other, asking them a million questions, pulling all-nighters poring over medical journals and googling for a cure or even just a diagnosis, researching alternative medicine as a possible option. What the gravity of the situation called for, we assumed, was near-superhuman effort. But such an approach would have been unsustainable, while also producing disappointing results.

Mercifully, we took the second path. We realized that the best way to help our daughter, and our whole family, through this time was not by exerting *more* effort. In fact, it was quite the opposite. We needed to find ways to make every day a little *easier*. Why? Because we needed to be able to sustain this effort for an unknown length of time. It was not negotiable: we simply could not now or ever burn out. If your job is to keep the fires burning for an indefinite period of time, you can't throw all the fuel on the flames at the beginning.

So we decided there were things we wouldn't do. Things we couldn't do. This situation was hard enough without *us* making it harder.

We wouldn't torture ourselves with unanswerable questions.
We wouldn't worry ourselves sick by imagining worst-case scenarios.
We wouldn't complain that the doctors didn't have the answers.
We wouldn't live in denial or tell ourselves, "It's not so bad."
We wouldn't try to force the timetable.
We wouldn't ask, "Why us?"
We wouldn't overanalyze every article from medical journals that well-intentioned people sent to us.
We wouldn't try to do it alone.

Instead, we decided to focus on the simple things, the easy things, the things we could control:

We got around the piano and sang.
We went on walks.
We read books.
We played games.
We looked for the positive and pointed it out.
We prayed together.
We ate dinner together.
We toasted each other.
We told stories.
We laughed.
We were grateful.

We did these things each day, and immediately we noticed an almost magical force at play. We felt less burdened. We were less exhausted. We didn't burn out.

Of course, the worry didn't disappear entirely. There were still doctors' appointments to be kept, test results to be waited for. Some days were harder than others. There were plenty of tears. But through it all there was also singing, laughing, eating, and making memories. We didn't just get through this difficult period, didn't just survive it. Our experience was gentler than that. From the moment we decided to choose the easier path, we felt somehow freer and lighter.

If this story were a Disney movie, this would be the part where I'd write about how Eve was healed and we all lived happily ever after. But after a round of successful treatments, she started to regress. The troubles returned. How could we have dealt with this setback had we depleted all our energy the first time around?

It's been two years now. Eve continues to get better. She still has some ways to go, but as I write this we have reason to believe she will be completely healed. She smiles, laughs, and jokes. She walks, runs, and wrestles. She reads, she writes. She is thriving again.

What did I learn from this experience?

Whatever has happened to you in life. Whatever hardship. Whatever pain. However significant those things are. They pale in comparison to the power you have to choose what to do now.

The word *now* comes from a Latin phrase, *novus homo,* which means "a new man" or "man newly ennobled." The spirit of this is clear: each new moment is a chance to start over. A chance to make a new choice.

Just think how the trajectory of a life can shift in the most fleeting of moments. The moments where we take control: "I choose," "I decide," "I promise," or "From now on. . . ." The moments we let go of emotional burdens: "I forgive you," "I am thankful," or "I'm willing to accept that." Or the moments when we make something right: "Please forgive me," "Let's start over," "I won't give up on you," or "I love you." In each new moment, we have the power to shape all subsequent moments.

Whatever has happened to you in life. Whatever hardship. Whatever pain. . . . They pale in comparison to the power you have to choose what to do now.

In each moment, we have a choice: Do I choose the heavier or the lighter path?

We watched our daughter diminish into a shell of her former self—and return from it. This is the personal experience that inspired me to write this book. To put into words what we learned, what we gained. To share with you the principles and practices of how to lighten our essential journey in life.

If you take away just one message from this book, I hope it is this: life doesn't have to be as hard and complicated as we make it. Each of us has, as Robert Frost wrote, "promises to keep, / And miles to go before I sleep." No matter what challenges, obstacles, or hardships we encounter along the way, we can always look for the easier, simpler path.

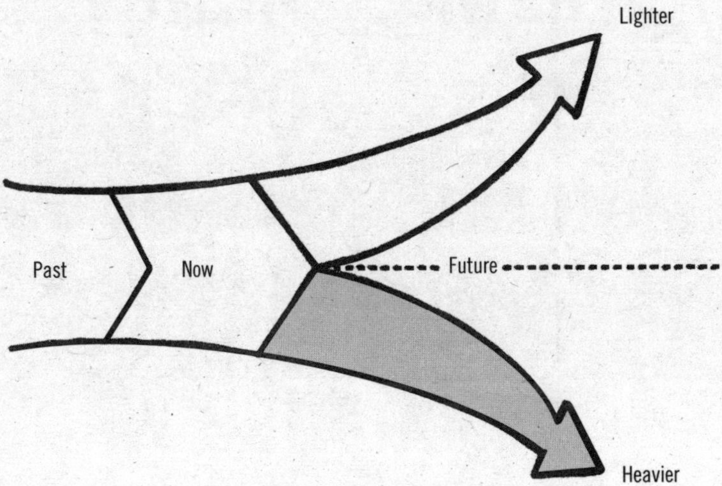

Acknowledgments

This book has been years in the making. And there are many people who have made it possible. I feel deep gratitude to the following people especially:

Thank you Anna Elizabeth McKeown. There is not one word in this book that doesn't have your fingerprint on it. You create a culture around you where things grow and thrive. I simply cannot imagine having this, or any, book without you. For discussing one hundred different titles—and then some. For enabling me to write. For aspiring with me to create a family culture where what is most essential becomes effortless. Thank you, forever.

Thank you to my children: Grace, Eve, Jack, and Esther. You have been such wonderful sounding boards all the way through the years leading to the completion of this book. You have heard every version of the book's title and subtitle, and have given good counsel. Ditto for the cover designs. Every reader of this book owes you each a debt of gratitude for making this book less and less rubbish. Thank you also for your permission to share your stories with other people. In some cases, they are personal and, to me, sacred. I share them here on the belief that they may be a blessing to others. Thank you.

Thank you to my extended family, especially as the book was

wrapping up, for reading the book and giving feedback: but even more than that, for your overall enthusiasm and encouragement. That has meant the world to me. The process has been made more special for it. Really: thank you.

Thank you to Rafe Sagalyn for being the greatest literary agent I could ever have hoped for. I love our conversations and insights. I am thankful for your consistent support for many years now. Thank you.

Thank you, Talia Krohn. What can I say? It has been one of the joys of my professional life to have you as my editor on *Essentialism* and *Effortless*. It has been a real pleasure to "go into" the document and work together on it. It's been like a scene from Harry Potter: to see improvements happening in real time. But it's been magic in other ways too. The fact that I already miss working on this project with you says it all. Thank you.

Thank you Jonathan Cullen for being such a great addition to "Team Effortless." You have been a class act, seriously. Your research and collaboration, your belief in the project, and your willingness to look for stories that surprise and delight have been thoroughly welcome: thank you.

Thank you to the many of you who read the manuscript and gave feedback. I'm thinking of you Sam Bridgstock, Neil Devor, Steve Hall, Nancy Josephson, Soraya Hold, Jade Koyle, Jim Meeks, Jason Peery, Jennifer Reid, Harry Reynolds, and Jeremy Utley.

Thank you to Terri Radstone for such excellent graphical support on the many cover versions: we got to the right place and I have so valued working with you. And to Denisse Leon for great support on the internal graphics and for the enthusiasm you bring to everything you do.

Thank you to the Essentialist Tribe the world over: readers, listeners, and colleagues. You give me fire for the deed each day. My goal has not been to write a book; it has been to write a book *for you*.

Finally, I want to acknowledge the hand of the Lord in anything that has been successful in this process. His words take on new meaning at the end of this deep dive into what *Effortless* really means. Breathtakingly, He said: "For my yoke is *easy*, and my burden is *light*" (Matt. 11:30).

Notes

Introduction. Not Everything Has to Be So Hard

3 **Let me tell you the story:** Patrick McGinnis, *The 10% Entrepreneur: Live Your Startup Dream Without Quitting Your Day Job* (New York: Portfolio/Penguin, 2016), 3–12. This is also based on my interviews with Patrick in August 2020.

4 **"I will work harder":** There are many editions of George Orwell's *Animal Farm,* but Boxer the Horse is described at the beginning of chapter 3 as a strong laborer whose answer to every problem is "I will work harder!," which he adopts as his personal motto. At the end of chapter 9, Boxer tries to utter these words even as he is weakened and dying.

12 **Since writing *Essentialism:*** Greg McKeown, *Essentialism: The Disciplined Pursuit of Less* (New York: Crown, 2014). Readers who want to design a more essential life can visit essentialism.com.

17 **like using special polarized sunglasses:** "How Do Polarized Sunglasses Work?," *SciShow,* August 11, 2018, YouTube, https://www.youtube.com/watch?v=rKlZ_ibIBgo.

19 **"What do we live for":** I have used the slightly modified version of the quote that is better known on various quotation sites; the original is "What do we live for, if it is not to make life less difficult to each other?" George Eliot, *Middlemarch: A Study of Provincial Life,* pt. 8, chap. 72; in Blackwood's 1872 edition, vol. 4, pp. 180–81. George Eliot was the pen name of the Victorian-era English poet and novelist Mary Ann Evans. Her famous remark reads in full: "Mr Lydgate would understand that if his friends hear a calumny about him their first wish must be to justify him. What do we live for, if it is not to make life less difficult to each other? I cannot be indifferent to the troubles of a man who advised me in my trouble, and attended me in my illness."

Part I: Effortless State

23 **The best free throw shooter ever:** Donne describes her secret in Brian Martin, "Elena Delle Donne Is the Greatest Free Throw Shooter Ever," WNBA, September 7, 2018, https://www.wnba.com/news/elena-delle-donne-is-the-greatest-free-throw-shooter-ever/. In 2019, Donne joined only eight NBA men in the prestigious 50-40-90 club (50 percent field goals, 40 percent three-point shooting, and 90 percent free throws in a season). Scott Allen, " 'Insane Numbers': NBA Stars Welcome Elena Delle Donne to 50-40-90 Club," *Washington Post,* September 9, 2019.

23 **Under optimal conditions:** Carl Zimmer, "The Brain: What Is the Speed of Thought?," *Discover,* December 16, 2009, https://www.discovermagazine.com/mind/the-brain-what-is-the-speed-of-thought. Zimmer concludes: "Faster than a bird and slower than sound. But that may be besides the point: Efficiency and timing seem to be more important anyway."

24 **perceptual load theory:** Nilli Lavie and Yehoshua Tsal, "Perceptual Load as a Major Determinant of the Locus of Selection in Visual Attention," *Perception and Psychophysics* 56, no. 2 (1994): 183–97.

24 **over six thousand thoughts a day:** Anne Craig, "Discovery of 'Thought Worms' Opens Window to the Mind," *Queen's Gazette,* July 13, 2020, https://www.queensu.ca/gazette/stories/discovery-thought-worms-opens-window-mind.

24 **And because our brains are programmed:** A. Tsouli, L. Pateraki, I. Spentza, and C. Nega, "The Effect of Presentation Time and Working Memory Load on Emotion Recognition," *Journal of Psychology and Cognition* 2, no. 1 (2017): 61–66. Participants were shown photographs of fearful, angry, happy, and neutral faces during a working memory load task. The study found that while the participants were able to efficiently recognize happy and neutral expressions without drawing on their working memory, negative faces created longer reaction times. The results suggest that we are hardwired to more automatically recognize friendly people in our environment but that when we encounter threats we begin to draw on working memory to more properly assess them.

1. Invert: What If This Could Be Easy?

27 **"I'm up photoshopping pictures":** Kimberly Jenkins, correspondence spanning from September 2019–June 2020.

29 **"blood, sweat, and tears":** "The Long History of the Phrase 'Blood, Sweat, and Tears,' " Word Histories, accessed October 15, 2020, https://wordhistories.net/2019/03/28/blood-sweat-tears/. This abbreviated version of the phrase became popular after Winston Churchill delivered a speech to the British House of Commons on May 13, 1940, having just replaced Neville Chamberlain as prime minister. He warned that he had "nothing to offer but blood, toil, tears and sweat." The original metaphor dates to the early seventeenth century, when the English poet John Donne wrote, "It with thy Teares, or Sweat, or Bloud: no thing" in *An Anatomy of the World: Wherein, by Occasion of the Untimely Death of Mis-*

tris Elizabeth Drury, the Frailty and the Decay of this Whole World Is Represented (London, 1611).

30 ***cognitive ease principle:*** Daniel Kahneman, *Thinking, Fast and Slow* (New York: Farrar, Straus and Giroux, 2013), chap. 5.

32 **"One must invert, always invert":** Edward B. Van Vleck, "Current Tendencies of Mathematical Research," *Bulletin of the American Mathematical Society* 23, no. 1 (1916): 1–14. The American mathematician Edward Burr Van Vleck wrote in 1916 of Jacobi's approach: "It was by turning the elliptic integral inside out that Jacobi obtained his splendid theory of elliptic and theta functions."

34 **The abolitionist William Wilberforce:** Robert Isaac Wilberforce and Samuel Wilberforce, *The Life of William Wilberforce* (London: John Murray, 1838). Wilberforce's antislavery efforts, which began in 1787, are well chronicled in this biography, published five years after his death by his two sons. In a letter to Reverend Thomas Clarkson, he called it "the greatest cause which ever engaged the efforts of public men" (*Life,* vol. 5, p. 44). However, that same year, his faith that he would achieve his goal waned, writing to Lord Muncaster on April 5, "As for my Foreign Slave Bill, I have, I confess, no hopes of its getting through the Lords, yet I do not relish its being suffered to lie upon the shelf."

A full view of all of his efforts over decades appears in the preface of *Life,* entitled "Tabular View of the Abolition of Slavery and the Slave Trade" (5:50).

34 **In 1805, Stephen wrote a pamphlet:** James Stephen, *War in Disguise; or, the Frauds of the Neutral Flags* (London: J. Hatchard, 1805), archive.org/details/warindisguiseorf00step/page/4/mode/2up?q=neutral.

35 **Beginning in January 1807:** Tom Holmberg, "The Acts, Orders in Council, &c. of Great Britain [on Trade], 1793–1812," Napoleon Series, 1995–2004, https://www.napoleon-series.org/research/government/british/decrees/c_britdecrees1.html. An order in council in the UK is a decree by the sovereign on the advice of the Privy Council. Unlike legislation, it does not require parliamentary approval. All of the 1807 orders in council can be found at this website.

35 **was formally outlawed:** An Act for the Abolition of the Slave Trade, 47 Georgii III, Session 1, cap. XXXVI. While it became illegal to sell and buy slaves in the British Empire after the coming into force of the act in 1807, slavery itself continued for a generation. It was finally outlawed on August 28, 1833, by An Act for the Abolition of Slavery throughout the British Colonies; for promoting the Industry of the manumitted Slaves; and for compensating the Persons hitherto entitled to the Services of such Slaves (more commonly known as the Slavery Abolition Act of 1833). Together, both pieces of legislation are known as the "Abolition Acts."

36 **Southwest cofounder Herb Kelleher:** T. D. Klein, *Built for Change: Essential Traits of Transformative Companies* (Santa Barbara, Calif.: Praeger, 2010), 51. The author recounts how Kelleher told this story to a small group early in Klein's career.

36 **Marketing author Seth Godin:** Tim Ferriss, *Tools of Titans: The Tactics, Routines, and Habits of Billionaires, Icons, and World-Class Performers*

(Boston: Houghton Mifflin Harcourt, 2016). The quote from Seth Godin appears on page 239 and that of Reid Hoffman on page 230.

37 **Arianna Huffington:** Arianna Huffington, *The Sleep Revolution: Transforming Your Life, One Night at a Time* (New York: Harmony Books, 2016), 4.

38 **Warren Buffett:** Warren E. Buffett, "Shareholder Letter," in *Berkshire Hathaway 1990 Annual Report* (Omaha: Berkshire Hathaway Inc., 1991), https://www.berkshirehathaway.com/letters/1990.html.

2. Enjoy: What If This Could Be Fun?

41 **the British activist Jane Tewson:** Based on my interview with Jane and our subsequent correspondence, June–August 2020.

41 **"I want to do right but not right now":** Gillian Welch, "Look at Miss Ohio," *Soul Journey*, Acony Records, 2003.

42 **Comic Relief is best known:** See "Red Nose Day 1980s," Comic Relief, n.d., accessed September 18, 2020, comicrelief.com/red-nose-day-1980s/, for the history of Comic Relief Red Nose Day.

42 **it's since become a biannual ritual:** "Comic Relief Raises £1bn over 30-Year Existence," BBC News Online, March 14, 2015.

44 **"the dark playground":** Tim Urban, "Why Procrastinators Procrastinate," *Wait But Why*, October 30, 2013, waitbutwhy.com/2013/10/why-procrastinators-procrastinate.html. Urban's clever stick-figure illustrations and insights have made his *Wait But Why* one of the Internet's most interesting blogs. This particular post reads in part: "The Dark Playground is a place every procrastinator knows well. It's a place where leisure activities happen at times when leisure activities are not supposed to be happening. The fun you have in the Dark Playground isn't actually fun because it's completely unearned and the air is filled with guilt, anxiety, self-hatred, and dread."

45 **Ron Culberson is good at many things:** "How to Make Difficult Tasks More Fun," *HuffPost*, October 26, 2012, https://www.huffpost.com/entry/enjoying-life_b_2009016. Ron Culberson styles himself a "funny speaker" and began his career by working with people at the end of their lives as a home care social worker. Also see https://ronculberson.com and Culberson's book *Do It Well. Make It Fun: The Key to Success in Life, Death, and Almost Everything in Between* (Austin, Tex.: Greenleaf Book Group, 2012).

49 **Take Ole Kirk Christiansen:** "The LEGO Group History," n.d., accessed September 21, 2020, lego.com/en-us/aboutus/lego-group/the-lego-group-history/. For more history of the LEGO Group, see "Automatic Binding Bricks," n.d., accessed September 21, 2020, lego.com/en-us/lego-history/automatic-binding-bricks-09d1f76589da4cb48f01685e0dd0aa73.

49 **"world's most powerful brand":** Kathryn Dill, "Lego Tops Global Ranking of the Most Powerful Brands in 2015," *Forbes*, February 19, 2015, https://www.forbes.com/sites/kathryndill/2015/02/19/lego-tops-global-ranking-of-the-most-powerful-brands-in-2015/#38a1825b26f0.

50 **Rituals are similar to habits:** "Dan Ariely: The Truth About Lies," *The*

Knowledge Project podcast, May 25, 2018, https://theknowledgeproject.libsyn.com/irrationality-bad-decisions-and-the-truth-about-lies.

51 **"The act of folding":** Marie Kondo, *The Life-Changing Magic of Tidying Up: The Japanese Art of Decluttering and Organizing* (Berkeley, Calif.: Ten Speed Press, 2014), 73.

51 **how Agatha Christie wrote:** Hilary Macaskill, *Agatha Christie at Home* (London: Frances Lincoln, 2014). The author describes how Christie bought her property in the late 1930s for £6,000. She had an architect renovate it, telling him, "I want a big bath and I need a ledge because I like to eat apples." In *The Agatha Christie Miscellany* (Cheltenham, UK: History Press, 2013), Cathy Cook writes: "Christie said she did her best thinking while lying in the bath, eating apples and drinking tea. She claimed that modern baths weren't made with authors in mind as they were 'too slippery, with no nice wooden ledge to rest pencils and paper on.'" Also see "The Blagger's Guide to: Agatha Christie," *Independent,* March 30, 2013, https://www.independent.co.uk/arts-entertainment/books/features/the-blaggers-guide-to-agatha-christie-8555068.html.

51 **Beethoven prepared his coffee:** Edmund Morris, *Beethoven: The Universal Composer* (New York: Atlas/HarperCollins, 2005), 80. Morris recounts how Beethoven chained together a series of rituals, including that of the morning coffee bean count: "At Unterdöbling [Beethoven's home], he fell into the annual routine he would pursue for the rest of his life; spring, summer, and early fall spent sketching music in the woods or wine country, winter in the city rendering his sketches into finished compositions. Thus the season of growth became associated in his mind with creativity, and leafless days with copying tryouts, rehearsals, concerts, and contracts. Throughout the year, he rose at dawn, breakfasted and brewed himself the strongest possible coffee (carefully counting out sixty beans per cup), then worked till midday at his 'piano desk' which allowed him to write and play at the same time."

51 **prone to devise a ritual:** Anthony Everitt, *Augustus: The Life of Rome's First Emperor* (New York: Random House, 2006), 120.

3. Release: The Power of Letting Go

53 **Fully dressed in an authentic Stormtrooper costume:** For those of you who, after careful reflection, would like to purchase an authentic Stormtrooper costume, I understand that the "Supreme Edition Stormtrooper Adult Costume" is available on Amazon for upwards of $1,000 (though more moderately priced versions are also available). Even better, children's versions are less expensive and perhaps more likely to meet the expectations of the wearer.

54 **the story of one Maître Hauchecorne:** Guy de Maupassant, "The Piece of String," Project Gutenberg, gutenberg.org/files/3090/3090-h/3090-h.htm#2H_4_0132, originally published in his short story collection *Miss Harriet* (Paris: Victor Havard, 1884).

57 **The *broaden-and-build theory:*** Barbara L. Fredrickson, "The Broaden-

and-Build Theory of Positive Emotions," *Philosophical Transactions of the Royal Society of London. Series B, Biological Sciences* 359, no. 1449 (September 29, 2004): 1367–78.

60 **"You're pushing no harder":** Jim Collins, *Good to Great: Why Some Companies Make the Leap . . . and Others Don't* (New York: Harper Business, 2001), 165.

60 **"Two turns . . . then four . . . then eight":** Jim Collins, *Turning the Flywheel: A Monograph to Accompany Good to Great* (New York: Harper Business, 2019), 1.

61 **He calls this a habit recipe:** BJ Fogg, *Tiny Habits: The Small Changes That Change Everything* (Boston: Houghton Mifflin Harcourt, 2019), 6.

62 **Chris Williams knew what mattered:** Chris Williams, *Let It Go: A True Story of Tragedy and Forgiveness* (Salt Lake City: Shadow Mountain, July 30, 2012).

64 **Rather, they "hire" them:** Clayton Christensen, *Competing Against Luck: The Story of Innovation and Customer Choice* (New York: Harper Business, 2016), 15. Christensen gives the delightful example of a fast-food chain that wanted to sell more milkshakes: "It turned out that a surprising number of milk shakes were sold before 9:00 a.m. to people who came into the fast-food restaurant alone. It was almost always the only thing they bought. They didn't stop to drink it there; they got into their cars and drove off with it. So we asked them: 'Excuse me, please, but I have to sort out this puzzle. What job were you trying to do for yourself that caused you to come here and hire that milk shake?' . . . It soon became clear that the early-morning customers all had the same job to do: they had a long and boring drive to work. They needed something to keep the commute interesting."

64 **Like Wormtongue in service to the king of Rohan in *The Lord of the Rings*:** J.R.R. Tolkien, *The Two Towers: Being the Second Part of The Lord of the Rings* (London: Allen and Unwin, 1954). Gríma Wormtongue is at first a faithful servant and adviser to King Théoden. But he later aligns himself with Rohan's secret enemy, the wizard Saruman, whose dark magic controls the king through Wormtongue's influence. As Gandalf describes the situation to Théoden, "And ever Wormtongue's whispering was in your ears, poisoning your thought, chilling your heart, weakening your limbs, while others watched and could do nothing, for your will was in his keeping." Tolkien was an accomplished linguist, and the name Gríma derives from the Old English or Icelandic word meaning "mask, visor, helmet" or "specter." "Gríma," Tolkien Gateway, n.d., accessed September 21, 2020, tolkiengateway.net/wiki/Gríma.

65 **It was this: "Hire slow, fire fast":** For more on this rule of thumb, see my "Hire Slow, Fire Fast," *Harvard Business Review,* March 3, 2014.

65 **my friend Jonathan Cullen:** This account is based on my many discussions with Jonathan over the course of writing this book in 2020. Tristan is happy and healthy, based on all the pictures his proud father keeps insisting on sending me.

66 **Maya Angelou:** "One of the Most Important Lessons Dr. Maya Angelou

Ever Taught Oprah," uploaded to YouTube May 19, 2014, https://www.youtube.com/watch?v=nJgmaHkcFP8.

66 **"For after all":** Henry Wadsworth Longfellow, "The Poet's Tale" in *Tales of a Wayside Inn* (Boston: Ticknor and Fields, 1863).

4. Rest: The Art of Doing Nothing

68 **Joe Maddon:** Paul Sullivan, "Joe Maddon's Unconventional Style Has Made Him the Toast of Chicago," *Chicago Tribune*, September 29, 2016, https://www.chicagotribune.com/sports/ct-cubs-joe-maddon-managerial-style-spt-0930-20160929-story.html, and Carrie Muskat, "Maddon Shakes Things Up with American Legion Week," Major League Baseball, August 20, 2015, https://www.mlb.com/news/cubs-joe-maddon-american-legion-week/c-144340696.

70 **Incredibly, over a five-year period:** Tony Andracki, "American Legion Week Has Come at a Perfect Time for the Cubs," NBC Sports, August 20, 2019, https://www.nbcsports.com/chicago/cubs/american-legion-week-has-come-perfect-time-cubs-nicholas-castellanos-rizzo-maddon-wrigley-field-little-league-world-series.

70 **the best-performing athletes, musicians, chess players:** K. A. Ericsson, R. T. Krampe, and C. Tesch-Römer, "The Role of Deliberate Practice in the Acquisition of Expert Performance," *Psychological Review* 100, no. 3 (July 1993): 363–406. This is the study that formed the basis for Malcolm Gladwell's ten-thousand-hour rule, although the study authors later claimed their results were misinterpreted; K. A. Ericsson, "Training History, Deliberate Practice and Elite Sports Performance: An Analysis in Response to Tucker and Collins Review—What Makes Champions?," *British Journal of Sports Medicine* 47 (2013): 533–35.

71 **Katrín Davíðsdóttir:** DaKari Williams, "Katrin Tanja Davidsdottir Plays Mental Game to Win CrossFit Games," ESPN, July 29, 2015, https://www.espn.com/espnw/athletes-life/story/_/id/13337513/katrin-tanja-davidsdottir-plays-mental-game-win-crossfit-games. This account is also based on my interview with Ben Bergeron in July 2020 and "How Katrin Davidsdottir Won the CrossFit Games," episode 65 of Bergeron's show *Chasing Excellence*, March 25, 2019, YouTube, https://www.youtube.com/watch?v=u_oNz-uwFW4.

72 **Collectively we all are:** D. A. Calhoun and S. M. Harding, "Sleep and Hypertension External," *Chest* 138, no. 2 (2010): 434–43.

73 **people who got less than six hours:** Hans P. A. Van Dongen, Greg Maislin, Janet M. Mullington, and David F. Dinges, "The Cumulative Cost of Additional Wakefulness: Dose-Response Effects on Neurobehavioral Functions and Sleep Physiology from Chronic Sleep Restriction and Total Sleep Deprivation," *Sleep* 26, no. 2 (March 2003): 117–26. The study authors concluded, "Sleepiness ratings suggest that subjects were largely unaware of these increasing cognitive deficits, which may explain why the impact of chronic sleep restriction on waking cognitive functions is often assumed to be benign."

73 **"Routine nightly sleep":** " 'Sleep Debts' Accrue When Nightly Sleep Totals Six Hours or Fewer; Penn Study Finds People Respond Poorly, While Feeling Only 'Slightly' Tired," *ScienceDaily*, March 14, 2003, https://www.sciencedaily.com/releases/2003/03/030314071202.htm.

73 **Sean Wise:** Sean Wise, "I Changed My Sleeping Habits for 30 Days, Here's How It Made Me a Better Entrepreneur," *Inc.*, September 14, 2019, https://www.inc.com/sean-wise/i-changed-my-sleeping-habits-for-30-days-heres-how-it-made-me-a-better-entrepreneur.html.

74 **This is not surprising:** Brian C. Gunia, "The Sleep Trap: Do Sleep Problems Prompt Entrepreneurial Motives but Undermine Entrepreneurial Means?," *Academy of Management Perspectives* 32 (June 13, 2018): 228–42.

74 **Having seen firsthand:** A. Williamson, M. Battisti, Michael Leatherbee, and J. Gish, "Rest, Zest, and My Innovative Best: Sleep and Mood as Drivers of Entrepreneurs' Innovative Behavior," *Entrepreneurship Theory and Practice* 483, no. 3 (September 25, 2018): 582–610.

74 **Healthy adults spend an average:** Jennifer Leavitt, "How Much Deep, Light, and REM Sleep Do You Need?," Healthline, October 10, 2019, https://www.healthline.com/health/how-much-deep-sleep-do-you-need.

74 **Uninterrupted sleep is when our brain waves:** Institute of Medicine, US Committee on Sleep Medicine and Research, and H. R. Colten and B. M. Altevogt, eds., *Sleep Disorders and Sleep Deprivation: An Unmet Public Health Problem* (Washington, D.C.: National Academies Press, 2006), 2.

75 **water-based passive body heating:** Shahab Haghayegh, Sepideh Khoshnevis, Michael H. Smolensky, Kenneth R. Diller, and Richard J. Castriotta, "Before-Bedtime Passive Body Heating by Warm Shower or Bath to Improve Sleep: A Systematic Review and Meta-analysis," *Sleep Medicine Reviews* 46 (2019): 124–35.

75 **naps can improve performance:** C. E. Milner and K. A. Cote, "Benefits of Napping in Healthy Adults: Impact of Nap Length, Time of Day, Age, and Experience with Napping," *Journal of Sleep Research* 18, no. 2 (2009): 272–81.

76 **They can improve mood, making us less impulsive and frustrated:** J. R. Goldschmied, P. Cheng, K. Kemp, L. Caccamo, J. Roberts, and P. J. Deldin, "Napping to Modulate Frustration and Impulsivity: A Pilot Study," *Personality and Individual Differences* 86 (2015): 164–67.

76 **a nap was as beneficial:** S. Mednick, K. Nakayama, and R. Stickgold, "Sleep-Dependent Learning: A Nap Is as Good as a Night," *Nature Neuroscience* 6, no. 7 (2003): 697–98.

76 **Ron Chernow tells the story:** Ron Chernow, *Grant* (New York: Penguin, 2017), 376. Ulysses S. Grant's exploits were often compared during his lifetime to those of Napoleon. Grant had an encyclopedic knowledge of his French counterpart's military tactics and apparently also his sleep patterns.

77 **Salvador Dalí's best-known painting:** Salvador Dalí, *The Persistence of Memory*, 1931, Museum of Modern Art, moma.org/collection/works/79018. The MoMA website offers an audio description of Dalí's painting and what he called "the usual paralyzing tricks of eye-fooling."

77 **Dalí's influences:** Ian Gibson, *The Shameful Life of Salvador Dalí* (London: Faber and Faber, 1997), chaps. 2 and 3.

77 **the surrealist version of a nap:** Drake Baer, "How Dali, Einstein, and Aristotle Perfected the Power Nap," *Fast Company,* December 10, 2013, https://www.fastcompany.com/3023078/how-dali-einstein-and-aristotle-perfected-the-power-nap.

78 **Dalí explained:** Salvador Dalí, *50 Secrets of Magic Craftsmanship* (Mineola, N.Y.: Courier Corporation, 2013), 37.

78 **"slumber with a key":** Baer, "How Dali, Einstein, and Aristotle."

5. Notice: How to See Clearly

79 **Sir Arthur Conan Doyle's character:** Guinness World Records News, "Sherlock Holmes Awarded Title for Most Portrayed Literary Human Character in Film and TV," Guinness World Records, May 14, 2012, https://www.guinnessworldrecords.com/news/2012/5/sherlock-holmes-awarded-title-for-most-portrayed-literary-human-character-in-film-tv-41743/?fb_comment_id=10150968618545953_27376924.

79 **"A Scandal in Bohemia":** In Doyle's *Adventures of Sherlock Holmes,* gutenberg.org/files/1661/1661-h/1661-h.htm.

81 **Left untreated, cataracts:** "Cataracts," The Mayo Clinic, accessed October 14, 2020, https://www.mayoclinic.org/diseases-conditions/cataracts/symptoms-causes/syc-20353790.

82 **Steph Curry had always dreamed:** "The Life and Times of Warriors' Star Stephen Curry," *GameDay News,* June 19, 2019, https://www.gamedaynews.com/athletes/life-of-stephen-curry/?chrome=1.

82 **trainer Brandon Payne:** "Every Exercise Steph Curry's Trainer Makes Him Do," GQ Sports: The Assist, September 20, 2019, YouTube, https://www.youtube.com/watch?v=M0FwbaLVHpg.

82 **"Steph Curry Literally Sees the World Differently":** Drake Baer, "Steph Curry Literally Sees the World Differently Than You Do," *The Cut,* June 13, 2016, https://www.thecut.com/2016/06/steph-curry-perception-performance.html.

83 **But even more useful:** "Dr. Jocelyn Faubert on NeuroTracker," TEDxMontreal, July 4, 2018, YouTube, https://www.youtube.com/watch?v=i7rz1dyZyi8.

84 **data on the intricate workings of relationships:** "John and Julie Gottman," Gottman Institute, n.d., accessed September 22, 2020, https://www.gottman.com/about/john-julie-gottman/.

84 **According to the Gottmans:** John Gottman and Joan DeClaire, *The Relationship Cure* (New York: Crown, 2002), chap. 2.

85 **as Eckhart Tolle has said:** "Eckhart Tolle and Peter Russell on Meditation," February 20, 2013, YouTube, https://www.youtube.com/watch?v=xDlnkNu0au0.

85 **Ronald Epstein felt his anxiety spike:** Ronald Epstein is a professor of family medicine, psychiatry, and oncology, University of Rochester School of Medicine and Dentistry, Rochester, New York. He is the author of *Attending: Medicine, Mindfulness and Humanity* (New York: Scribner, 2017).

87 **the Clearness Committee:** "Clearness Committees—What They Are and What They Do," FGC Friends General Conference, n.d., accessed September 22, 2020, https://www.fgcquaker.org/resources/clearness-committees-what-they-are-and-what-they-do.

88 **As Parker Palmer, an expert:** Parker J. Palmer, "The Clearness Committee: A Communal Approach to Discernment in Retreats," Center for Courage & Renewal, accessed October 14, 2020, http://www.couragerenewal.org/clearnesscommittee/.

Part II: Effortless Action

95 **the movement of millions of free throws:** Robbie Gonzalez, "Free Throws Should Be Easy. Why Do Basketball Players Miss?," *Wired*, March 28, 2019, https://www.wired.com/story/almost-impossible-free-throws/.

95 **law of *diminishing returns*:** Adam Hayes, "Law of Diminishing Marginal Returns," Investopedia, August 24, 2020, https://www.investopedia.com/terms/l/lawofdiminishingmarginalreturn.asp.

97 **This is an example of overexertion:** Viktor Frankl used a similar term, *hyperintention,* for especially extreme cases in his patients. But I like the term *overexertion* for the general populace.

98 ***wu wei:*** Harry J. Stead, "The Principle of Wu Wei and How It Can Improve Your Life," *Medium,* May 14, 2018, https://medium.com/personal-growth/the-principle-of-wu-wei-and-how-it-can-improve-your-life-d6ce45d623b9.

6. Define: What "Done" Looks Like

99 **Four hundred years ago, Gustav II:** Pablo Lledó, "Wasa and Scope Creep—Based on a True Story," trans. Dr. David Hillson, accessed October 15, 2020, http://pablolledo.com/content/articulos/WASA%20-%20Scope%20Creep.pdf. See also Eric H. Kessler, Paul E. Bierly III, and Shanthi Gopalakrishnan, "Vasa Syndrome: Insights from a 17th-Century New-Product Disaster," *The Academy of Management Executive* 15, no. 3 (August 2001): 80–91, https://www.jstor.org/stable/4165762?seq=1. The vessel is known both as the *Wasa* and *Vasa*.

104 **Swedish Death Cleaning:** Margareta Magnusson, *The Gentle Art of Swedish Death Cleaning: How to Free Yourself and Your Family from a Lifetime of Clutter* (New York: Scribner, 2018).

7. Start: The First Obvious Action

107 **Today, Netflix is found:** Alex Sherman, "Netflix Has Replaced Broadcast TV as the Center of American Culture—Just Look at the Viewership Numbers," CNBC, April 21, 2020, https://www.cnbc.com/2020/04/21/netflix-massive-viewership-numbers-proves-it-owns-pop-culture.html#:~:text=Netflix%20has%20more%20than%20183%20million%20global%20subscribers.

107 **Hastings's idea was to build Netflix:** "Keynote 4: Reed Hastings, CEO and Founder, Netflix," Mobile World Congress 2017, February–March 2017, Mobile World Live, https://www.mobileworldlive.com/mobile-world-congress-2017.

108 **"That was the moment":** Jon Xavier, "Netflix's First CEO on Reed Hastings and How the Company Really Got Started | Executive of the Year 2013," *Silicon Valley Business Journal,* January 8, 2014, https://www.bizjournals.com/sanjose/news/2014/01/08/netflixs-first-ceo-on-reed-hastings.html Also see Alyssa Abkowitz, "How Netflix Got Started," *Fortune,* January 28, 2009, https://archive.fortune.com/2009/01/27/news/newsmakers/hastings_netflix.fortune/index.htm.

109 **Productivity expert April Perry:** "Four Unbelievably Simple Steps to Double Your Productivity," *Learn Do Become,* accessed October 15, 2020, https://learndobecome.com/wp-content/uploads/2016/11/Four-Unbelievably-Simple-Steps-Transcript.pdf?inf_contact_key=cb4c4e5fef9fce1717df2acfb975a1f352696a354c5a36f7c65eb862cc3ca8f2.

110 **Konmari Method:** Marie Kondo, *The Life-Changing Magic of Tidying Up: The Japanese Art of Decluttering and Organizing* (Berkeley, Calif.: Ten Speed Press, 2014), 12.

110 **An alternative is offered by Fumio Sasaki:** Fumio Sasaki, *Goodbye, Things: The New Japanese Minimalism* (New York: Norton, 2017), 87.

110 **Eric Ries:** Eric Ries, "Minimum Viable Product: A Guide," *Startup Lessons Learned,* August 3, 2009, http://soloway.pbworks.com/w/file/fetch/85897603/1%2B%20Lessons%20Learned_%20Minimum%20Viable%20Product_%20a%20guide2.pdf.

111 **the founders of Airbnb:** Rebecca Aydin, "How 3 Guys Turned Renting Air Mattresses in Their Apartment into a $31 Billion Company, Airbnb," *Business Insider,* September 20, 2019, https://www.businessinsider.com/how-airbnb-was-founded-a-visual-history-2016-2.

111 **"Though she be but little she is fierce":** William Shakespeare, *A Midsummer Night's Dream* (Signet Classics), ed. Wolfgang Clemen (New York: Signet, 1998).

111 **A microburst is a meteorological:** "What Is a Microburst?," National Weather Service, accessed October 15, 2020, https://www.weather.gov/bmx/outreach_microbursts#:~:text=A%20microburst%20is%20a%20localized,%2C%20can%20be%20life%2Dthreatening.

111 **A microburst in April Perry's vernacular:** April Perry, "[Podcast 53]: How to Utilize Pockets of Time," June 6, 2019, *Learn Do Become,* https://learndobecome.com/episode53/.

112 **the "now" we experience lasts only 2.5 seconds:** Laura Spinney, "The Time Illusion: How Your Brain Creates Now," *New Scientist,* January 7, 2015. The author first introduced me to this measurement. She in turn is quoting Marc Wittmann, founder of the Marc Wittmann Institute for Frontier Areas of Psychology and Mental Health in Freiburg, Germany. Wittmann said, "Your sense of nowness underpins your entire conscious experience."

8. Simplify: Start with Zero

115 **Peri Hartman:** Conversation with Peri Hartman, April 17, 2020.

116 **"They should be able to click on one thing":** Richard L. Brandt, *One Click: Jeff Bezos and the Rise of Amazon.com* (New York: Portfolio/Penguin, 2011).

116 **Amazon filed a patent:** Mike Arsenault, "How Valuable Is Amazon's 1-Click Patent? It's Worth Billions," *Rejoiner,* accessed October 15, 2020, http://rejoiner.com/resources/amazon-1clickpatent/.

120 **A tiny but pivotal moment:** Louis V. Gerstner, Jr., *Who Says Elephants Can't Dance* (New York: Harper Business, 2003), 43.

121 **"Then you click the button that says BURN":** Farhad Manjoo, "Invincible Apple: 10 Lessons from the Coolest Company Anywhere," *Fast Company,* July 1, 2010, https://www.fastcompany.com/1659056/invincible-apple-10-lessons-coolest-company-anywhere.

124 **"Manifesto for Agile Software Development":** Jim Highsmith, "History: The Agile Manifesto," Agile Alliance, 2001, agilemanifesto.org/history.html.

124 **As sportswriter Andy Benoit observes:** Andy Benoit, *Andy Benoit's Touchdown 2006: Everything You Need to Know About the NFL This Year* (New York: Ballantine Books, July 14, 2006).

9. Progress: The Courage to Be Rubbish

125 **a British industrialist named Henry Kremer:** Anthony Morris, "A Willingness to Fail Solved the Problem of Human-Powered Flight," *Financial Review,* October 6, 2015, https://www.afr.com/work-and-careers/management/being-willing-to-fail-solved-the-problem-of-humanpowered-flight-20151016-gkb658.

126 **"no matter how ugly it is":** Paul MacCready and John Langford, "Human-Powered Flight: Perspectives on Processes and Potentials," MIT 1998 Gardner Lecture, uploaded to YouTube November 13, 2019, https://www.youtube.com/watch?v=t8C8-BB_7nw.

127 **"We all start out ugly":** A version of this article appeared in the April 2014 issue of *Fast Company* magazine: Ed Catmull, "Lessons from Pixar President Ed Catmull: Your Ideas Are 'Ugly Babies,' You Are Their Champion," https://www.fastcompany.com/3027548/pixars-ed-catmull-on-the-importance-of-protecting-new-ideas.

128 **"greenhousing" protects their early ideas:** John Klick, "Culture Eats Strategy: Using It to Your Advantage to Inspire Innovation Action," *PDS Blog,* October 1, 2018, https://www.pdsxchange.com/2018/10/culture-eats-strategy-using-it-to-your-advantage-to-inspire-innovation-action/.

130 **"In order to move fast":** Ben Casnocha, "Reid Hoffman's Two Rules for Strategy Decisions," *Harvard Business Review,* March 5, 2015, https://hbr.org/2015/03/reid-hoffmans-two-rules-for-strategy-decisions.

130 **"If you're not embarrassed":** Reid Hoffman, "Imperfect Is Perfect," *Masters of Scale* podcast, Ep. 4, May 24, 2017, https://mastersofscale.com/mark-zuckerberg-imperfect-is-perfect/.

131 **Irish playwright:** George Bernard Shaw, *The Doctor's Dilemma: Preface on Doctors* (New York: Brentano's, 1911), lxxxv and lxxxvi, https://babel.hathitrust.org/cgi/pt?id=mdp.39015008017934&view=1up&seq=3.

132 **"A word after a word after a word":** Chris Knight, "Chris Knight: 'A Word after a Word after a Word Is Power' Is a Celebration of All Things Atwoodian," *National Post,* November 6, 2019, https://nationalpost.com/entertainment/movies/chris-knight-a-word-after-a-word-after-a-wordis-power-is-a-celebration-of-all-things-atwoodian.

10. Pace: Slow Is Smooth, Smooth Is Fast

133 **the most sought-after goal:** Roland Huntford's *The Last Place on Earth: Scott and Amundsen's Race to the South Pole* (New York: Atheneum, 1983) tells the story in exquisite detail.

136 **She was prolific:** Conversation with Janice Kapp Perry, May 10, 2020. See also Susan Easton Black and Mary Jane Woodger, *Women of Character: Profiles of 100 Prominent LDS Women* (American Fork, Utah: Covenant Communications), 227–29.

137 **Lisa Jewell:** Lucy Moore, "Before I Met You by Lisa Jewell," *Female First,* May 23, 2013, https://www.femalefirst.co.uk/books/before-i-met-you-292526.html.

137 **Ben Bergeron is a former Ironman triathlete:** This account is based on my interview with Ben Bergeron in July 2020.

139 **VUCA:** Paul Shoemaker, "Can You Handle VUCA? If You Can't, You Could Perish," *Inc.,* September 27, 2018, https://www.inc.com/paul-schoemaker/can-you-vuca.html.

139 **"Slow is smooth. Smooth is fast":** Joe Indvik, "Slow Is Smooth, Smooth Is Fast: What SEAL and Delta Force Operators Can Teach Us About Management," LinkedIn, November 24, 2015, https://www.linkedin.com/pulse/slow-smooth-fast-what-seal-delta-force-operators-can-teach-joe-indvik/.

Part III: Effortless Results

149 **Steve Nash still holds the record:** Robbie Gonzalez, "Free Throws Should Be Easy. Why Do Basketball Players Miss?," *Wired,* March 28, 2019, https://www.wired.com/story/almost-impossible-free-throws/.

152 **Benjamin Franklin summarized the idea:** Burton Malkiel and Charles Ellis, *The Elements of Investing: Easy Lessons for Every Investor* (Hoboken, NJ: Wiley, 2013), 11. "When Franklin died in 1790, he left a gift of $5,000 to each of his two favorite cities, Boston and Philadelphia. He stipulated that the money was to be invested and could be paid out at two specific dates, the first 100 years and the second 200 years after the date of the gift. After 100 years, each city was allowed to withdraw $500,000 for public works projects. After 200 years, in 1991, they received the balance—which had compounded to approximately $20 million for each city."

152 **Jessica Jackley:** Jessica Jackley, *Clay, Water, Brick: Finding Inspiration*

from Entrepreneurs Who Do the Most with the Least (New York: Random House, 2015). Also based on correspondence with Jessica in July 2020.

153 **Archimedes, the Greek mathematician:** Diodorus Siculus, *Diodorus Siculus: Library of History,* vol. 11, books 21–32, trans. Francis R. Walton (Cambridge, Mass.: Harvard University Press, 1957).

11. Learn: Leverage the Best of What Others Know

155 **Galileo Galilei, the father of observational astronomy:** A. Storr, "Issac Newton," *British Medical Journal (Clinical Research Edition)* 291, no. 6511 (1985): 1779–84.

156 **the word *principia* means:** "Principia," Classic Thesaurus, accessed October 15, 2020, https://www.classicthesaurus.com/principia/define.

156 **Harrington Emerson, the American efficiency engineer:** George N. Lowrey Company, "The Convention: Fifteenth Annual Convention of the National Association of Clothiers, Held June 5 and 6, 1911," *The Clothier and Furnisher* 78, no. 6 (1911): 86.

157 **Peter Kaufman:** "The Three Buckets of Knowledge," *FS Blog,* February 2016, https://fs.blog/2016/02/three-buckets-lessons-of-history/.

158 **Christmas cards to almost six hundred complete strangers:** P. R. Kunz and M. Woolcott, "Season's Greetings: From My Status to Yours," *Social Science Research* 5, no. 3 (1976): 269–78.

159 **He was once asked how:** See AMA ("Ask Me Anything") question-and-answer session with Elon Musk on Reddit, January 5, 2015, https://www.reddit.com/r/IAmA/comments/2rgsan/i_am_elon_musk_ceocto_of_a_rocket_company_ama/. Musk writes, "I think most people can learn a lot more than they think they can. They sell themselves short without trying. One bit of advice: it is important to view knowledge as sort of a semantic tree—make sure you understand the fundamental principles, ie the trunk and big branches, before you get into the leaves/details or there is nothing for them to hang on to."

Unrelatedly, when asked later in the exchange by another user, "What daily habit do you believe has the largest positive impact on your life?" Musk responded simply, "Showering."

160 **Neuroplasticity is our brain's ability to change:** Patrice Voss, Maryse E. Thomas, J. Miguel Cisneros-Franco, and Étienne de Villers-Sidani, "Dynamic Brains and the Changing Rules of Neuroplasticity: Implications for Learning and Recovery," *Frontiers in Psychology* 8, no. 1657, https://psycnet.apa.org/record/2017-47425-001.

160 **achieved returns of over 24 percent:** Robert Abbot, "Big Mistakes: Charlie Munger," *Guru Focus,* July 1, 2019, https://www.gurufocus.com/news/902508/big-mistakes-charlie-munger.

161 **Isaiah Berlin's original 1953 essay:** Isaiah Berlin, *The Hedgehog and the Fox* (London: Weidenfeld & Nicolson, 1953).

161 **Jim Collins famously favored:** Jim Collins, *Good to Great: Why Some Companies Make the Leap and Others Don't* (New York: Harper Business, 2001), 90.

161 **Munger's approach to investing:** Tren Griffin, *Charlie Munger: The Complete Investor* (New York: Columbia Business School Publishing, 2015), 43.

161 **Northwestern University's Kellogg School of Management:** B. Uzzi et al., "Atypical Combinations and Scientific Impact," *Science* 342, no. 6157 (2013): 468–72.

162 **Joel and Ethan Coen's first blockbuster film:** "Hidden Connections Conference," Nanyang Technological University, Singapore, March 31, 2015, YouTube, https://www.youtube.com/watch?v=mbxcAFh4wO8.

163 **four books a year:** Andrew Perrin, "Slightly Fewer Americans Are Reading Print Books, New Survey Finds," Pew Research Center, October 19, 2015, https://www.pewresearch.org/fact-tank/2015/10/19/slightly-fewer-americans-are-reading-print-books-new-survey-finds/. This survey also found that seven-in-ten American adults (72 percent) had read a book within the past year, whether in whole or in part and in any format (down from 79 percent). Happily, this number rises to 80 percent among adults aged 18–29, proving that contrary to popular opinion, millennials do in fact read.

163 **Use the Lindy Effect:** "How to Choose Your Next Book," *FS Blog*, August 2013, https://fs.blog/2013/08/choose-your-next-book/.

164 **high jumper Dick Fosbury:** Avi Charkham, "You're Not a Two-Legged Camel You're Just Different," *Medium*, January 18, 2019, https://medium.com/@aviche/two-legged-camel-9e60eb09eb57. See also "How One Man Changed the High Jump Forever, the Olympics on the Record," April 1, 2018, YouTube, https://www.youtube.com/watch?v=CZsH46Ek2ao.

12. Lift: Harness the Strength of Ten

169 ***Project*Protect, a collaboration among various community groups:** https://projectprotect.health/#/.

171 **Aesop was a storyteller:** "Aesop," *Britannica*, accessed October 15, 2020, https://www.britannica.com/biography/Aesop.

173 **"Sesame Street Simple":** Robert Sutton and Huggy Rao, *Scaling Up Excellence: Getting to More Without Settling for Less* (New York: Random House Business, 2016). Sutton and Rao attribute this principle to former Procter and Gamble CEO A. G. Lafley, who believes that "his Sesame Street–simple slogans, repeated over and over, keep everyone trained on what's important." Five-year-olds everywhere agree.

13. Automate: Do It Once and Never Again

176 **"Civilization advances by extending":** Alfred North Whitehead, *An Introduction to Mathematics* (London: Williams and Norgate, 1911), 61.

177 **Major Hill's tragic oversight:** Atul Gawande, *The Checklist Manifesto: How to Get Things Right* (New York: Metropolitan Books, 2009), 33.

177 **Humans have a tremendous capacity:** Paul Reber, "What Is the Memory Capacity of the Human Brain?," *Scientific American*, May 1, 2010, https://www.scientificamerican.com/article/what-is-the-memory-capacity/.

179 **Stephen and Irene Richards:** https://www.legacy.com/obituaries/saltlaketribune/obituary.aspx?n=irene-gaddis&pid=170495784&fhid=11607.

180 **"Admittedly I was a bit careless":** Alexander Sehmer, "Teenager's Parking Appeals Website Saves Motorists £2m After Overturning Thousands of Fines," *Independent,* December 29, 2015, https://www.independent.co.uk/news/uk/home-news/teenager-s-parking-appeals-website-saves-motorists-ps2m-after-overturning-thousands-fines-a6789711.html. See also https://donotpay.com/ and "Meet the Teen Taking on the Parking Ticket," BBC News, September 6, 2015, https://www.bbc.co.uk/programmes/p031rmqv.

181 **In 2012, leaders at Expedia:** Dan Heath, "How Expedia Solved a $100 Million Customer Service Nightmare," *Medium,* March 3, 2020, https://marker.medium.com/how-expedia-solved-a-100-million-customer-service-nightmare-d7aabc8d4025. Ryan O'Neill confirmed this account to me in a conversation in August 2020.

14. Trust: The Engine of High-Leverage Teams

186 **Closed the McLane deal:** Warren Buffett, "Chairman's Letter," February 27, 2004, Berkshire Hathaway, Annual Report, p. 6, https://berkshirehathaway.com/letters/2003ltr.pdf.

188 **Steve Hall, a successful entrepreneur:** Based on a conversation with Hall on August 25, 2020.

189 **Warren Buffett uses three criteria:** "Warren Buffett Speaks with Florida University," YouTube, October 15, 1998, uploaded to YouTube July 3, 2013, https://www.youtube.com/watch?v=2MHIcabnjrA&t=1050s.

190 **"When people trust you":** Kim Scott, *Radical Candor: Fully Revised & Updated Edition: Be a Kick-Ass Boss Without Losing Your Humanity* (New York: St. Martin's Publishing Group, 2019), 9.

192 **Lean Construction Institute:** Accessed October 15, 2020, https://www.leanconstruction.org/.

15. Prevent: Solve the Problem Before It Happens

195 **In 1977, Ali Maow Maalin was a hospital cook:** Alexis C. Madrigal, "The Last Smallpox Patient on Earth: The Case of Ali Maow Maalin, a Somalian Cook," *The Atlantic,* December 9, 2013, https://www.theatlantic.com/health/archive/2013/12/the-last-smallpox-patient-on-earth/282169/.

196 **John opened a desk drawer:** David Allen, *Getting Things Done: The Art of Stress-Free Productivity* (New York: Penguin Books, 2015), 237. As David Allen adds, when describing what he called "this simple but extraordinary next-action technique," his longtime friend and management consulting mentor Dean Acheson is of no relation to the former secretary of state.

198 **"There are a thousand hacking at the branches":** Henry David Thoreau, *Walden* (New York: Thomas Y. Crowell, 1910), 98.

199 **Suddenly, Mary's heart stopped:** Michael A. Roberto, *Know What You*

Don't Know: How Great Leaders Prevent Problems Before They Happen (Upper Saddle River, NJ: Pearson Education, 2009), 1.

201 **In 2014, the French satirical newspaper:** "French Red Faces over Trains That Are 'Too Wide,'" BBC News, May 20, 2014, https://www.bbc.com/news/world-europe-27497727. See also "French Trains Are Too Wide for Stations," NPR, May 22, 2014, https://www.npr.org/2014/05/22/314925114/french-trains-are-too-wide-for-stations.

Conclusion. Now: What Happens Next Matters Most

213 **"promises to keep, / And miles to go before I sleep":** Robert Frost, "Stopping by Woods on a Snowy Evening," in *New Hampshire* (New York: Henry Holt, 1923).

Index

Chapter 1

The Essentialist

The wisdom of life consists in the elimination of non-essentials.

—*Lin Yutang*

Sam Elliot* is a capable executive in Silicon Valley who found himself stretched too thin after his company was acquired by a larger, bureaucratic business.

He was in earnest about being a good citizen in his new role so he said *yes* to many requests without really thinking about it. But as a result he would spend the whole day rushing from one meeting and conference call to another trying to please everyone and get it all done. His stress went up as the quality of his work went down. It was like he was majoring in minor activities and as a result, his work became unsatisfying for him *and* frustrating for the people he was trying so hard to please.

* Name has been changed.

In the midst of his frustration the company came to him and offered him an early retirement package. But he was in his early 50s and had no interest in completely retiring. He thought briefly about starting a consulting company doing what he was already doing. He even thought of selling his services back to his employer as a consultant. But none of these options seemed that appealing. So he went to speak with a mentor who gave him surprising advice: "Stay, but do what you would as a consultant and nothing else. And don't tell anyone." In other words, his mentor was advising him to do only those things that *he* deemed essential—and ignore everything else that was asked of him.

The executive followed the advice! He made a daily commitment toward cutting out the red tape. He began saying no.

He was tentative at first. He would evaluate requests based on the timid criteria, "Can I actually fulfill this request, given the time and resources I have?" If the answer was *no* then he would refuse the request. He was pleasantly surprised to find that while people would at first look a little disappointed, they seemed to respect his honesty.

Encouraged by his small wins he pushed back a bit more. Now when a request would come in he would pause and evaluate the request against a tougher criteria: "Is this the very *most* important thing I should be doing with my time and resources right now?"

If he couldn't answer a definitive *yes,* then he would refuse the request. And once again to his delight, while his colleagues might initially seem disappointed, they soon began to respect him *more* for his refusal, not less.

Emboldened, he began to apply this selective criteria to everything, not just direct requests. In his past life he would always volunteer for presentations or assignments that came up last minute;

now he found a way to not sign up for them. He used to be one of the first to jump in on an e-mail trail, but now he just stepped back and let others jump in. He stopped attending conference calls that he only had a couple of minutes of interest in. He stopped sitting in on the weekly update call because he didn't need the information. He stopped attending meetings on his calendar if he didn't have a direct contribution to make. He explained to me, "Just because I was invited didn't seem a good enough reason to attend."

It felt self-indulgent at first. But by being selective he bought himself space, and in that space he found creative freedom. He could concentrate his efforts on one project at a time. He could plan thoroughly. He could anticipate roadblocks and start to remove obstacles. Instead of spinning his wheels trying to get everything done, he could get the right things done. His newfound commitment to doing only the things that were truly important—and eliminating everything else—restored the quality of his work. Instead of making just a millimeter of progress in a million directions he began to generate tremendous momentum toward accomplishing the things that were truly vital.

He continued this for several months. He immediately found that he not only got more of his day back at work, in the evenings he got even more time back at home. He said, "I got back my family life! I can go home at a decent time." Now instead of being a slave to his phone he shuts it down. He goes to the gym. He goes out to eat with his wife.

To his great surprise, there were no negative repercussions to his experiment. His manager didn't chastise him. His colleagues didn't resent him. Quite the opposite; because he was left only with projects that were meaningful to him *and* actually valuable to the company, they began to respect and value his work more than ever. His work became fulfilling again. His performance ratings went up. He ended up with one of the largest bonuses of his career!

In this example is the basic value proposition of Essentialism: only once you give yourself permission to stop trying to do it all, to stop saying yes to everyone, can you make your highest contribution toward the things that really matter.

What about you? How many times have you reacted to a request by saying yes without really thinking about it? How many times have you resented committing to do something and wondered, "Why did I sign up for this?" How often do you say yes simply to please? Or to avoid trouble? Or because "yes" had just become your default response?

Now let me ask you this: Have you ever found yourself stretched too thin? Have you ever felt both overworked *and* underutilized? Have you ever found yourself majoring in minor activities? Do you ever feel busy but not productive? Like you're always in motion, but never getting anywhere?

If you answered yes to any of these, the way out is the way of the Essentialist.

The Way of the Essentialist

Dieter Rams was the lead designer at Braun for many years. He is driven by the idea that almost everything is noise. He believes very few things are essential. His job is to filter through that noise until he gets to the essence. For example, as a young twenty-four-year-old at the company he was asked to collaborate on a record player. The norm at the time was to cover the turntable in a solid wooden lid or even to incorporate the player into a piece of living room furniture.

Instead, he and his team removed the clutter and designed a player with a clear plastic cover on the top and nothing more. It was the first time such a design had been used, and it was so revolutionary people worried it might bankrupt the company because nobody would buy it. It took courage, as it always does, to eliminate the nonessential. By the sixties this aesthetic started to gain traction. In time it became the design every other record player followed.

Dieter's design criteria can be summarized by a characteristically succinct principle, captured in just three German words: *Weniger aber besser.* The English translation is: *Less but better.* A more fitting definition of Essentialism would be hard to come by.

The way of the Essentialist is the relentless pursuit of less but better. It doesn't mean occasionally giving a nod to the principle. It means pursuing it in a *disciplined* way.

The way of the Essentialist isn't about setting New Year's resolutions to say "no" more, or about pruning your in-box, or about mastering some new strategy in time management. It is about pausing constantly to ask, "Am I investing in the right activities?" There are far more activities and opportunities in the world than we have time and resources to invest in. And although many of them may be good, or even very good, the fact is that most are trivial and few are vital. The way of the Essentialist involves learning to tell the difference—learning to filter through all those options and selecting only those that are truly essential.

Essentialism is not about how to get more things done; it's about how to get the *right* things done. It doesn't mean just doing less for the sake of less either. It is about making the wisest possible investment of your time and energy in order to operate at our highest point of contribution by doing only what is essential.

Energy
Energy

The difference between the way of the Essentialist and the way of the Nonessentialist can be seen in the figure opposite. In both images the same amount of effort is exerted. In the image on the left, the energy is divided into many different activities. The result is that we have the unfulfilling experience of making a millimeter of progress in a million directions. In the image on the right, the energy is given to fewer activities. The result is that by investing in fewer things we have the satisfying experience of making significant progress in the things that matter most. The way of the Essentialist rejects the idea that we can fit it all in. Instead it requires us to grapple with real trade-offs and make tough decisions. In many cases we can learn to make one-time decisions that make a thousand future decisions so we don't exhaust ourselves asking the same questions again and again.

The way of the Essentialist means living by design, not by default. Instead of making choices reactively, the Essentialist deliberately distinguishes the vital few from the trivial many, eliminates the nonessentials, and then removes obstacles so the essential things have clear, smooth passage. In other words, Essentialism is a disciplined, systematic approach for determining where our highest point of contribution lies, then making execution of those things almost effortless.

The Model

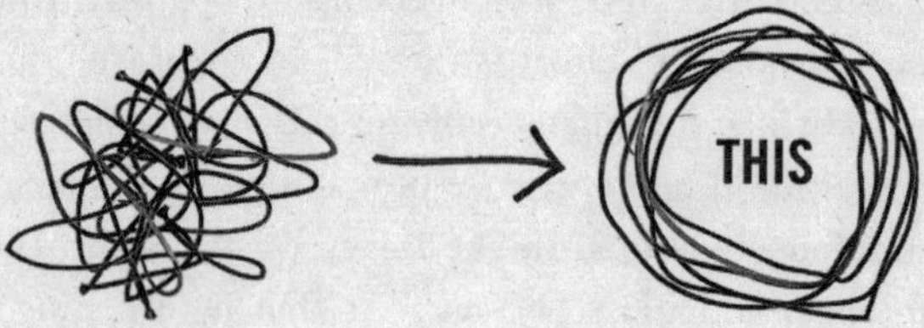

	Nonessentialist	Essentialist
Thinks	**ALL THINGS TO ALL PEOPLE** "I have to." "It's all important." "How can I fit it all in?"	**LESS BUT BETTER** "I choose to." "Only a few things really matter." "What are the trade-offs?"
Does	**THE UNDISCIPLINED PURSUIT OF MORE** Reacts to what's most pressing Says "yes" to people without really thinking Tries to force execution at the last moment	**THE DISCIPLINED PURSUIT OF LESS** Pauses to discern what really matters Says "no" to everything except the essential Removes obstacles to make execution easy
Gets	**LIVES A LIFE THAT DOES NOT SATISFY** Takes on too much, and work suffers Feels out of control Is unsure of whether the right things got done Feels overwhelmed and exhausted	**LIVES A LIFE THAT REALLY MATTERS** Chooses carefully in order to do great work Feels in control Gets the right things done Experiences joy in the journey

The way of the Essentialist is the path to being in control of our own choices. It is a path to new levels of success and meaning. It is the path on which we enjoy the journey, not just the destination. Despite all these benefits, however, there are too many forces conspiring to keep us from applying the disciplined pursuit of less but better, which may be why so many end up on the misdirected path of the Nonessentialist.

The Way of the Nonessentialist

On a bright, winter day in California I visited my wife, Anna, in the hospital. Even in the hospital Anna was radiant. But I also knew she was exhausted. It was the day after our precious daughter was born, healthy and happy at 7 pounds, 3 ounces.

Yet what should have been one of the happiest, most serene days of my life was actually filled with tension. Even as my beautiful new baby lay in my wife's tired arms, I was on the phone and on e-mail with work, and I was feeling pressure to go to a client meeting. My colleague had written, "Friday between 1–2 would be a bad time to have a baby because I need you to come be at this meeting with X." It was now Friday and though I was pretty certain (or at least I hoped) the e-mail had been written in jest, I still felt pressure to attend.

Instinctively, I knew what to do. It was clearly a time to be there for my wife and newborn child. So when asked whether I planned to attend the meeting, I said with all the conviction I could muster . . .

"Yes."

To my shame, while my wife lay in the hospital with our hours-old baby, I went to the meeting. Afterward, my colleague said, "The client will respect you for making the decision to be here." But the look on the clients' faces did not evince respect. Instead, they mirrored how I felt. *What was I doing there?* I had said "yes" simply to please, and in doing so I had hurt my family, my integrity, and even the client relationship.

As it turned out, exactly *nothing* came of the client meeting. But even if it had, surely I would have made a fool's bargain. In trying to keep everyone happy I had sacrificed what mattered most.

On reflection I discovered this important lesson:

If you don't prioritize your life, someone else will.

About the Author

Greg McKeown is the host of the *What's Essential* podcast, a business strategist, a public speaker, and a bestselling author. He has been featured in *The New York Times, Fast Company, Fortune, Politico,* and *Inc.*, and is among the most popular bloggers for *Harvard Business Review* and LinkedIn. McKeown has been interviewed on NPR, NBC, Fox, and *The Steve Harvey Show*. He serves as a Young Global Leader for the World Economic Forum.